BE

YOUR SELF

Discover the Power of Being Yourself

2 Manuscripts

The Power of Enneagram — The Power of Stoicism

JOHN TURNER

Table of Contents

Book 2 - The Power of Stoicism

The Power OF Enneagram

JOHN TURNER

Introduction

Thanks for choosing this book about Enneagram. I'd love to hear your opinion, so make sure to leave a short review on Amazon if you enjoy it. It means a lot to me!

Discover How to Better Understand Yourself and Others, Improving All Relationships". If you are reading this, it is because you are keen on learning more about yourself and those around you. It is highly likely that you have asked yourself on more than one occasion on what it takes to understand the people around you. Moreover, you are more than likely interested in finding a great way to improve your relationships with others in your social circle.

If you have found it difficult to relate to others, or simply want to improve how you communicate with the folks around you, then you have come to the right place. In this book, you will find a collection of thoughts, ideas, tips, and strategies about understanding yourself and those around you.

How is this possible?

With the power of the Enneagram of Personality, you will find a treasure trove of information that will not only help you better understand yourself but also better understand the way humans function in general.

Yes, that's right.

You don't need an advanced psychology degree to gain a good understanding of the way people act, and react, under given circumstances. The Enneagram has made it a lot simpler for the average individual to gain a solid grasp of how the human psyche works based on the various personality types that apply to people.

When you can fully comprehend the way your personality works, you can get a better sense of who you are concerning those you come in contact with regularly. Besides, this understanding of yourself will allow you to position yourself in such a way that you can along with others much more easily.

But that's not the only thing that understanding the Enneagram can do for you. When you understand the Enneagram, you can get a better sense of the way others around see the world and the way they react to the various circumstances they come into contact with. This is a powerful understanding as it allows you to make sense of the way people act and the reason why they do the things they do.

This is powerful stuff indeed.

As such, this book is intended for anyone who is looking to, firstly, gain a better understanding of who they are. Sure, there are plenty of personality tests out there. There is an abundance of information on personality types and so on. But the fact of the matter is that many of these tests are rather limited in their scope.

Then, you have complex personality tests such as the Myers-Biggs which requires training to administer it correctly. While this is no denying that proper examinations such as the Myers-Biggs are certainly valid, the fact remains that they are long, costly and require a considerable investment in terms of time.

Also, this book is intended for the individual who is looking to simply improve their relationships. These relationships can range from average workplace interactions to deeper and more meaningful relationships such as with family, close friends and romantic partners. After all, wouldn't it be great if you could truly understand what's going in someone else's head?

Sure, it is impossible to read minds, at least as far as we're concerned, but truthfully, when you understand the way an individual's personality is structured, you can have a solid lead as to what another person might be thinking.

Furthermore, this book is intended for anyone who is a student of human psychology and behavior. That is why the value that the study of the Enneagram provides is useful to gain a fresh perspective on what may seem like inexplicable reactions and behaviors on the part of those whom you come into contact with.

Now, you might be asking yourself, how can the Enneagram help me understand why others act the way they do?

The effectiveness in the Enneagram lies in the fact that it is a model of the human psyche. This model can create a representation of the human psyche through a series of personality types. Each personality type contains a set of traits that are inherent to that personality type. Thus, an individual of a given personality type will be expected to behave and react in a given manner. This makes human behavior far more predictable than you might have initially thought.

Additionally, your understanding of the Enneagram's personality types will help put your personality into focus. This is the starting point. When you can gain a deeper understanding of who you are and why you act the way you do, you will be able to put yourself into a much broader context. Then, your visualization of the remaining personality types will enable you to detect the behavioral patterns of such personality types in such a way that you will be able to anticipate the way individuals will react.

Of course, there is a great deal of science behind the Enneagram. But the great thing about it is that you don't have to go through a vast amount of work and study to get the most out of it. By reading this book thoroughly, you will be well on your way to unlocking the secrets of the Enneagram. You will be able to make the most of your newfound understanding of the various personality types.

By the end of this book, you will have answered plenty of questions you might have wrestled with previously. These answers will lead you to improved relationships, better opportunities and an improved sense of self.

You will find that this book has been written in a sequential manner that will allow you to go through all of the information about the study of the Enneagram in a digestible manner. It is easy to understand and written in a way which your reading will simply flow.

So, what are we waiting for?

Let's jump right on in.

Chapter 1

The Enneagram of Personality

We will kick things off with this chapter on what the Enneagram of Personality is, what it can be used for, and how you can apply it to your everyday life. It is important to remember that the practical applications of the Enneagram are meant to be within your rea-life, everyday context. We are not talking about some abstract, esoteric science that will leave you with more questions than answers. We are looking to focus on the practical aspects of the Enneagram which will help you get ahead in your pursuits.

The Enneagram of Personality is a model of the human psyche. That is what it boils down to. The Enneagram is intended to systematize the way the human mind works in such a way that seemingly random reactions and behaviors are part of a logical pattern that responds to a specific model that you can identify in every person you meet.

Hence, the Enneagram model is based on nine personality types. Each type has its traits which tend to dominate how an individual behaves. This means that the traits identified in each personality type would be considered as the predominant traits of an individual's personality.

Of course, nothing is black and white in life. There are nuances in every individual which make a clear-cut application of each personality type impossible. This means that every person will have a predominant personality type but will ultimately have traits of other types.

The combination of predominant traits and the influence of secondary traits are what make up the complex apparatus that is the human psyche. The patterns identified in each personality type will enable you to, firstly, gain a broad understanding of the way the psyche of a given person works. Then, the secondary traits observed in a person will shed more light on an individual's overall behavioral patterns.

It is important to note that how you can determine the various personality types is through the administration of a test. These tests consist of questions that can be answered in such a way that you can create a broad profile of an individual's mindset. The great thing about the Enneagram is that you won't have to administer complex tests that require special training to both administer and interpret.

The tests used to determine personality types based on the Enneagram of Personality are very straightforward and contain relevant information for both the test-take and the administrator. Moreover, these tests are simple enough and non-invasive. This is a stark contrast with most psychological evaluations in which test-takers are often bombarded with invasive questions. More often than not, test-takers dodge these questions thus leading to inaccurate results at the end of the examination.

A great place to start with Enneagram testing is https://enneagramtest.net/. In this website, you can find a short, non-invasive test that will reveal your predominant personality type. The test contained in this website can help you, and anyone interested in taking it, gain an introduction into the nine personality types.

A more comprehensive test based on the Riso-Hudson Enneagram Indicator can be found at https://www.9types.com/rheti/index.php. This test is slightly longer than the one found at enneagramtest.net and provides additional insight into the various personality types.

Also, the Enneagram Institute offers a similar type of test. This only difference is that this test is offered through professional evaluation services that have a cost attached to administering the test. Its results are believed to be the standard in terms of the Enneagram of Personality. As such, this could become an interesting option if you are keen on getting a professional assessment based on the Enneagram.

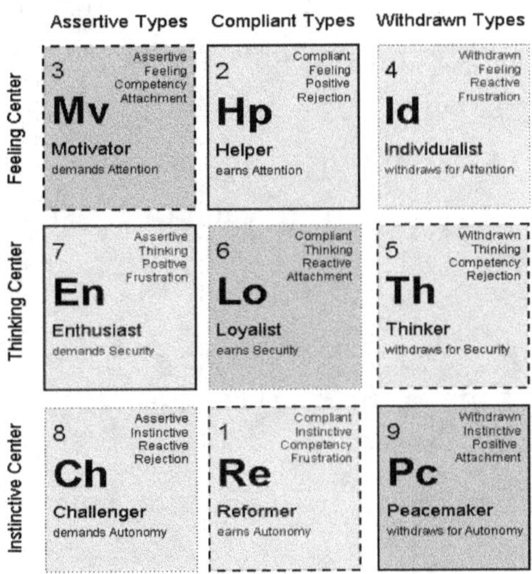

Source: Fitzel.ca

Based on the results obtained through the Enneagram test, one of the nine personality types can be identified for a test taker. Once again, it is worth noting that the main personality is determined based on the predominant traits observed in the individual.

As such, the Enneagram model poses nine personality types from which an individual can derive their main traits. Let's take a look at what these nine personality types are:

1.   The reformer/perfectionist
2.   The helper/giver
3.   The individualistic/performer
4.   The achiever/performer
5.   The investigator/observer
6.   The loyalist/skeptic
7.   The enthusiast/epicurist
8.   The challenger/protector
9.   The peacemaker/mediator

As you can see, each personality type is identified by a name made up of two general descriptors. This is intended to give you an idea of what the personality type is just by looking at the name. Naturally, there is far more to it than that. Nevertheless, it is possible to derive meaning from each one just by taking a cursory glance.

Naturally, when you delve deeper into each one of these items, the components that make up every one of these personality types reveals a profound level of understanding about how an individual will act, and react, in their day to day interactions with the world.

So, let's take a general overview of each of the personality types. We will be presenting a very concise description of each one.

Naturally, we will be taking an extensive look into each one in individual chapters.

- The reformer/perfectionist is the rational and idealistic kind. Type one is principled, purposeful, self-controlled, and perfectionistic.
- The helper/giver is the caring and interpersonal type. Type two is demonstrative, generous, people-pleasing, and possessive.
- The individualistic/performer is the success-oriented and pragmatic type. Type three is adaptive, excelling, driven, and image-conscious.
- The achiever/performer is a sensitive and withdrawn type. Type four is expressive, dramatic, self-absorbed, and temperamental.
- The investigator/observer is an intense and cerebral type. Type five is perceptive, innovative, secretive, and isolated.
- The loyalist/skeptic is the committed and security-oriented type. Type six is engaging, responsible, anxious, and suspicious.
- The enthusiast/epicurist is the busy and fun-loving type. Type seven is spontaneous, versatile, distractible, and scattered.
- The challenger/protector is a powerful and dominating type. Type eight is self-confident, decisive, willful, and confrontational.
- The peacemaker/mediator is the easygoing and self-effacing type. Type nine is receptive, reassuring, agreeable, and complacent.

As you can see, the main descriptors for each personality type are very straightforward. If you would like to make a quick assessment of your personality type, read through each one of the types and choose the one that you feel best describes you. Based on this, you can get your first taste of the way the Enneagram of Personality works in real-life action.

The great thing about the Enneagram of Personality is that you can use these personality types to better position yourself within the social circle that finds yourself in. For example, companies use personality types to gain a better understanding of the people working in a single department. This is especially useful when team members aren't getting along.

As such, companies are willing to invest the time and money that it takes to implement the knowledge derived from the Enneagram. Also, companies administer the Enneagram test to know their candidates better during recruitment. Now, it should be noted that this isn't a question of using this test to filter out candidates. The main point of using this test is to see how a particular individual would fit into the organization.

Consequently, the Enneagram can be utilized to place individuals where they would best fit with the existing team members. In many ways, it's like being able to fit the parts of a machine to exact specifications.

Beyond recruitment, companies also use this test to repair broken-down relationships. This is especially true when departments or entire companies have trouble getting along. Often, companies have significant events, such as a merger or acquisition, in which relationships tend to deteriorate. In such cases, this test can help team members gain a better understanding of each other's behavioral patterns. What this does is highlight the fact that many of the reactions that people have are not a reflection of personal problems. Rather, they are just the effect of how an individual reacts to the circumstances surrounding them.

On a more personal level, the Enneagram is a great way of figuring family dynamics. For instance, some parents are having a hard time understanding their kids. Some families are having trouble relating to one another. Hence, the Enneagram is a way in which individuals can gain a deeper insight into themselves and their relatives. And just like the workplace, this enables folks to repair relationships and find the best way to communicate.

As you can see, the Enneagram is certainly a valuable tool when it comes to self-development and self-exploration. By understanding what makes you tick on a deeper level, you will be able to fully embrace who you are and why you do the things you do. When you reach that point, it is like playing the game of life in hack mode.

Chapter 2

Type One: The reformer/perfectionist

In this chapter, we are going to be diving in headfirst into the Type One personality which is known as the "Reformer" or the "Perfectionist". You will find most references to this type as the "Reformer" though you will also find some references as "perfectionist".

With this first type, there is a duality between change and perfection. As the name suggests, the Reformer is all about seeking change. However, it should be noted that this isn't about change for the sake of change. We are talking about change with a purpose.

As such, change with purpose refers specifically to finding constant improvement above all things. This is fueled by a dedicated and methodical work ethic that is hard to beat. Type One as organized, orderly and meticulous about the way they go about doing things. Thus, the perfectionist side of the personality type enables the individual to find the path to achieving improvement.

Type One is also driven by a high sense of morals. In that regard, they are driven by the principles and values they hold dear. This, in turn, becomes a guiding light for them in their quest for what they believe is right and wrong. It is not rare to see Reformers have a strong sense of duty and a clear differentiation of what is right and wrong.

The main fear of Type One is to become corrupted or defective. This has as much to do with compromising their morals as it does with their performance. Hence, a Reformer will find it hard to accept subpar performance. This personal commitment to performance can lead this personality type to put a considerable amount of pressure on themselves.

The main driving force, or desire, for the Reformer, is to be good, to have integrity and attain balance. Of course, this is easier said than done. Nevertheless, Type One strives to make its best effort in achieving what they believe to be fairness and justice.

Perhaps the most important thing to keep in mind with Type One is their intrinsic motivation to be right, to improve things, and to have things move along under the guidance of their principles. On the flip side, Type One doesn't take criticism too kindly. This is important to keep in mind as Reformers try to stay away from criticism that can lead to the judgment which, in turn, can lead to condemning a given attitude or behavior.

Notable Type Ones are Nelson Mandela, Joan of Arc and Michelle Obama among many other luminaries. These notable Types Ones are classic examples of how the Reformer is constantly seeking to bring about change while upholding the most virtuous values. In fact, as the case of Nelson Mandela, this type would rather endure prison than give up their beliefs. Joan of Arc lost her life over her beliefs. Michelle Obama brought about a revolution with grace and poise worth of a First Lady.

Considering how the Reformer is all about change, these individuals have made it their life's mission to change the world around, but not to suit their own, personal needs. Rather, they intend to change their surroundings in such a way that their values and principles are upheld at all costs.

This leads the Reformer to be incredibly idealistic. Of course, it should be noted that many of these values are culture-specific. For example, Nelson Mandela fought for a very different set of values than Joan of Arc. Granted, they lived centuries apart, and while their circumstances were completely different, their mission was the same: to rid the world of the tyranny they felt was unfairly oppressing their people.

As a result of this personal mission, Type One tends to be very results-oriented. What this means is that a Reformer's mission is guided by some tasks and results that need to be achieved. This could something as simple as organizing their local community to pushing major changes in national legislation.

Such monumental changes have been the result of the personal mission of a Reformer. A great example of this is Mahatma Gandhi. Like Nelson Mandela. Gandhi fought against an oppressive system that was unjustly punishing his people. Yet, the genius in Gandhi's resistance was a non-violent approach. This led to radical changes resulting in a transformational chain of events.

It is important to take into consideration that Reformers tends to be quite the perfectionist. This is due to their results-oriented nature. Since Reformers tend to be very organized and methodical, they will demand that things be done in a certain way as per their specifications. This can become a very negative trait if not properly addressed.

Consequently, one of the biggest challenges that Type One has to face is the fact that they can't control everything no matter how hard they try. This allows room for error. And while a Reformer simply cannot tolerate errors, the reformer needs to accept the fact that not everything can be "perfect".

This is why the "perfectionist" tag added to the name of this personality type is apt. In the worst of cases, the perfectionist personality can lead an individual to become demanding and even overbearing. As a result, the perfectionist needs to understand that they cannot control everything around them. This attitude may also lead to unfair expectations of others as they may hold others up to the same standards, they hold themselves up to.

It is important to note that this rather extreme attitude of the Reformer can develop over time particularly when the individual finds themselves in situations in which they have to overcome large amounts of adversity.

Nevertheless, when considering how Reformers hold themselves accountable for their actions, it is quite common to see these individuals think their actions through. Perfectionists are well aware that their actions have consequences. This is the reason why they tend to overthink the things they do. They feel that if they make a mistake, they may compromise their values, and by extension, their life's mission.

Now, it is also important to consider that the development of the Type One personality is based on levels. Each level indicates the degree of growth that the individual has attained. Thus, level 1 is the level at which the personality type is at its best while level 9 is where the least optimal level of performance can be found.

Types One loves to shoot for level 1. Since they are constantly seeking to improve, they will certainly take achieving level 1 very seriously.

In **level 1**, the Reformer is at their absolute best. At this point, the Reformer can understand that they cannot control everything. Also, they accept a certain degree of mistakes as they also understand how mistakes can be a learning experience as well.

As far as **level 2** goes, the Reformer is humane, polite, kind and helpful, among other things. They tend to be leaders though they may be too analytical and logical at times.

At **level 3**, values, commitment and a strong work ethic are the main driving force behind a Type One. They are focused and determined to achieve their goals.

Levels 1, 2, and 3 are considered to be healthy levels, that is, the level in which a regular person will exhibit their best traits.

In **level 4**, you may find Reformers' feelings dissatisfied or even disenfranchised. This can lead them to take matters into their own hands and become advocates and supporters of specific causes. They may also lead them to do volunteer work in the hope of changing the world for the better.

In **level 5** Reformers tend to be a bit too careful. They will not engage in any activities that are not aligned with their principles. Think of a politician that will or will not do an activity because they feel that it does not reflect their ideals.

In **level 6**, Reformers tend to get very judgmental or extremely picky with the things they do, the people they talk to and their expectations from those around them. At this level, they are very hard on themselves.

Levels 4 through 6 are considered to be "average" levels. But levels 7 through 9 are considered to be "unhealthy" levels as the negative traits of this personality type become more and more predominant.

For **level 7** Reformers, these individuals can become overbearing and patronizing as they feel they are the only ones who hold the truth. They can an incessant need to be right.

In **level 8** Reformers are more judgmental and can become obsessed with perfection. This is where "neat freaks" may emerge. They are also dogmatic in their beliefs.

In **level 9** Reformers are at the most complex level for this personality type. At this point, Reformers can show signs of depression. Also, they can become so obsessive that they can develop obsessive-compulsive disorder.

As you can see, the Reformer type is rather extensive. Also, they may become addicted to, or obsess, with cleanliness and order. Also, they may use alcohol as a coping mechanism for the wrongs they are unable to right.

So, here are some tips to consider for Type One who want to continue improving themselves:

- Relax. Don't take things too seriously. Of course, some situations must be treated very seriously. But in general, just try to relax a bit more.

- Teach. Reformers are usually great teachers. They love to show others how things can be done. Type One is a generally great teacher.

- Watch yourself. It may be very easy to spot the mistakes that others are making. But Type Ones needs to acknowledge that they are not perfect and make mistakes as well.

- Keep your emotions in check. Reformers may become highly emotional especially when they witness injustice or unfair treatment. While standing up and being vocal is important, letting emotion take over may lead to negative consequences.

Finally, it should be pointed out that Type One generally gets along with everyone. At the same time, they tend to grind up against virtually every other type. So, this means that a Type One should try to find a balance between their crusades and circumstances around them. They also need to recognize that we are all human and therefore make mistakes.

In a nutshell, Type One needs to live by their values but without making their will more important than that of others.

Chapter 3

Type Two: The Helper/Giver

In this chapter, we are going to focus on the personality type known as the "Helper". This personality type is also referred to as the "giver". Also, you will see this type referred to as Type Two.

As this type's name would suggest, the Helper is the type of individual who is focused on helping those around them regardless of the circumstances. They are the kind of person who is focused on making sure that others are happy and comfortable. Needless to say, these are folks who can be found in occupations that are geared toward helping others such as caregivers, paramedics and so on.

When Types Two are at their best, they are often selfless and altruistic. They are capable of exhibiting unconditional love. Most importantly, they are always focused on helping those in need. Under this type, you can picture humanitarian aid workers or folks who volunteer for charitable causes.

Some luminaries under the Types Two category include Pope John XXIII, Eleanor Roosevelt, and Bishop Desmond Tutu. These notable figures illustrate a penchant for humanitarian work, such as Eleanor Roosevelt, while exuding peace and compassion as seen in Pope John XXIII and Bishop Tutu.

By most standards, Types Two individuals are those who are first to offer help in times of need. There is no need to ask Types Two to volunteer. They are always ready, willing and able to give their time, effort and talents to causes they truly believe in.

Perhaps this is an underlying issue that needs to be considered. When Types Two truly believe in a cause, or if they see that a person genuinely needs help, they are willing to spring into action at a moment's notice. However, if they feel that the cause does not warrant their efforts, then they may refrain from being the first to enter the fray.

Types Two are the kind of folks who get personally involved in the lives of others… but in a good way. These are not the folks who show up for work every day and see people as numbers. They take a genuine interest in seeing people for what they are: people. A good example of these individuals are those caseworkers who go the extra mile, doctors who will call up patients to see how they are doing, or teachers who take a personal stake in the wellbeing of their students.

When Helpers are balanced and in sync with their life's mission, they are the most generous, loving, caring and compassionate individuals that you will find. Think of those humanitarian aid workers who are living in deplorable conditions, yet they feel fulfilled because they have found their true calling. They won't care about finding themselves in adverse conditions so long as they can help others in need.

However, the flip side of the incredibly loving personality type is an excessive involvement in others' lives. This may lead them to become overly nosy. They may even feel they have a right to tell others how to run their lives as they feel compelled to spare people from themselves. Needless to say, Types Two that finds themselves acting in this manner will cause more harm than good. After all, Types Two may have a hard time understanding the difference between people who need help and people who want to be helped. As such, if a person needs help, but is unwilling to cooperate, may spur a Types Two to become involved despite the other party's reluctance.

One of the biggest concerns for Types Two is a feeling of worthlessness, that is, they may become sad and depressed if they feel they are no use to anyone. This is rooted in the innermost need to be of service. Hence, Types Two biggest desire to serve others regardless of the circumstances. Consequently, their biggest fear is to be unable to serve and thereby become useless to their peers and those around them.

In return for the often, self-sacrificing attitude, Helpers seek some sort of validation. While these individuals offer their efforts without seeking anything in return, they do seek some sort of validation. For instance, they may become distraught if a person whom they wish to help refuses their offer. This lack of validation may lead a giver to feel reject and worthless.

As such, Types Two need to become focused on the fact that they do have a lot to offer to everyone around them. The difference may lie, however, in the way that others may perceive their value. This is where it becomes very difficult for Helpers to acknowledge the fact that not everyone is seeking their even if they do need it.

Nevertheless, when Types Two are allowed to shine, they will do so in the best possible way they can. You will not hear them complaining even if they are under stress and harsh conditions. They will rise to the occasion every time they are needed.

In terms of each level of development, Helpers will transition through various stages. Here is a breakdown of each level of development for this type.

In **level 1**, Types Two are extremely selfless, humble and will give their unconditional love and support to those who need it. These are family members who will stop at nothing to see their loved ones feel well. These are the employees that truly care about their company or business owners who take a genuine interest in their employees' wellbeing. Also, you will find teachers, doctors, lawyers and so on, who make each person their own, personal business.

In **level 2** Helpers are thoroughly empathetic, kind and supportive. They will be concerned about others' needs and wants. They are dedicated to the wellbeing of those around them. They will not take long to forgive someone for their faults.

At **level 3** Helper is a very positive and upbeat individual who is looking to serve others. They are active in their community. They exude love and care especially with those who need a helping hand. They often volunteer for charitable work.

Levels 1 to 3 are an example of how a Type Two will behave when in a healthy stage of development. The following levels, 4 to 6, reflect the way a Type Two would behave when situated in an average stage of development.

In **level 4**, Helpers are "people pleasers". This is, of course, a double-edged sword as people-pleasers are not always fulfilled in what they do. They often find themselves being stressed out over gaining people's approval and validation. Needless to say, this can grow into a rather complex situation. Nevertheless, folks at this stage are very friendly and helpful individuals.

At **level 5** Helpers can exhibit traits in which they are nosy and intrusive. They tend to meddle in other people's business. While this may not be as evident as in other individuals, they do take things far too personally. These folks feel compelled to tell others what to do.

In **level 6**, Givers begin to feel that they are the most important person in the world. These are the types who feel that a company cannot run without them, a family will crumble if they leave, or the world will stop if they are not around to solve things for others. This stems from a lack of validation in which they feel they are not getting the recognition they feel they deserve.

Next, the unhealthy levels show what a Type Two will act when they find themselves in a lower level of personal development.

In **level 7**, Helpers can become manipulative. They may guilt people into doing things. They may even engage in some type of substance abuse to cope with feeling though food tends to be their preferred coping mechanism.

In **level 8** Givers are bent on getting their way. They can be domineering and resort to coercive measures to get people to do what they want. They feel they ought to get repayment for their efforts and service to others.

Finally, **level 9** Types Two can find a logical explanation for the abuse they inflict on others. A classic example of this is an abusive parent that justifies such behavior on their child under the pretense of "disciplining" them. These individuals may end up suffering from chronic health issues as a result of the somatization of their unvalidated feelings. Their ultimate goal is to burden others to get the attention they seek.

In general terms, Types Two can find a path to growth in the following ways:

- You need to help yourself before you can help others. If you are not well, you will never be able to help others be well.

- Make sure you are clear of why you are helping others. Try to avoid disguising ulterior motives with an apparent selfless intention of serving others.

- It is very important to avoid seeking attention for your good deeds. While validation is important, it is also self-destructive to feel that you need recognition for every good deed you do. Often, the best deeds go unnoticed.

- Also, it is important to recognize others' sincere gratitude and their desire to be helped. A kind "thank you" can be validation enough when you help someone. By the same token, a person who does not wish to be helped needs to be left alone until they seek the help they need.

On the whole. Types Two are some of the most selfless and inspiring people in the world.

Chapter 4

Type Three: The Achiever/Performer

In this chapter, we are going to be taking a look at the "Achiever" personality type. We will also be referring to this personality type as Type Three. Furthermore, this personality type can also be referred to as the Performer type. This should not be confused with one other personality type that also carries the performer label. Nevertheless, they do hold striking similarities though they are completely different personality types.

This personality type, as its name indicates is all about getting results. This is the most pragmatic and success-oriented of the nine types in the Enneagram. These folks are very practical and will find the best and most efficient way to get things done. Period. While they enjoy the finer things in life, they are focused and driven by achieving the goals they have set out to accomplish at the outset of their endeavors.

When they are at their best, Type Threes are excellent executors. They are the kind of people that get things done. They can make the most of the resources they have while minimizing the time and effort it takes to make things happen.

The basic, underlying fear of Type Threes is a sense of worthlessness, that is, not being able to achieve what they set out to do in life thereby not contributing to themselves and their community. Thus, their biggest motivation is a sense of being valuable to themselves and those around them. This is what drives them to achieve as much as they can. Ultimately, they seek the recognition that comes with being the best in their fields or achieving great success, the likes of which, few people can accomplish.

Under this category, some of the most accomplished individuals come to mind. Some great examples are Boxer Muhammed Ali, former President Bill Clinton, Motivational speaker Tony Robbins, and golfer Tiger Woods.

As you can see by the exemplary individuals listed under this personality type, Type Threes are highly focused on getting results. Indeed, a pragmatic results-oriented approach is needed if you are going to be the most powerful person in the world, that is, the President of the United States. In the case of Tony Robbins, you can see how his work is geared toward helping people achieve what they want to get out of their lives. Furthermore, Tiger Woods is an example of how hard work and dedication can help you climb to the top of your respective field. As for Muhammed Ali, he becomes the best in his field despite humble beginnings. He was able to transform talent into success as a result of his efforts.

If you identify yourself under this personality type, then you can appreciate the value of hard work and dedication in achieving the goals that you have set out for yourself. It should be noted that it is not the goals and endeavors themselves that count, rather, it is the dedication and willingness to achieve them that makes the difference.

When Achievers are balanced and healthy, they are valuable members of their community insofar as their contributions help to make changes in their surroundings. These are the individuals who will make community events happen, get school fairs off the ground, or make charitable drives successful. They are very cheerful and upbeat about rolling up their sleeves and getting down to business.

However, the flipside of Type Threes is becoming too focused on outcomes and not on the people surrounding them. For example, they will value material possessions over family and measure success in terms of money rather than happiness. These folks can descend into workaholics who place very little value on their home life. They may also become frustrated when they don't get the results they expect. In their worst moments, they will be quick to dismiss people when they don't get the result they want before actually giving them a chance.

Hence, the balance between results and expectations is important for Achievers. Achievers, who are also performers, need to understand that not everyone is quite as driven as they are. Some folks would rather enjoy the ride regardless of how long it takes them to get there. It should be noted that Type Threes are performers because they are all about doing. Achievers who play team sports are known for being great leaders who push their teammates to achieve their collective goals.

Let's take a look at how Type Threes act and react based on their level of personal development.

Firstly, healthy levels 1 to 3 reflect the following attitudes:

In **level 1**, Achievers are authentic, self-accepting and focused. They are very humble and modest folks who have a great sense of humor. They value teamwork and collective success.

In **level 2** Achievers are highly self-confident and competent people. These are the best bosses you could ever work for as they are focused on helping others become the best they can be. They are creative in finding solutions to common obstacles to getting results.

For **level 3,** Achievers' ambition is a great driving force, that is, positive ambition. This ambition is manifested in their desire to achieve change, reach their goals and be the best they could be. These individuals are highly admired for the results they can get in their chosen field.

Now, let's take a look at average levels of development, that is, levels 4 to 6.

Level 4 Achievers are highly competent individuals. These are very efficient employees who are driven to reach their personal and corporate goals. However, the underlying driving forces in level 4 Achievers is more a fear of failure rather than a desire to achieve.

In **level 5**, Achievers are more concerned about the way they are perceived by others as opposed to doing things out of their desire. As such, their wish to be successful is based more on their social status rather than doing what they wish to do for themselves. These are typical social climbers.

For a **level 6** Achiever, their drive is to impress others. These are folks who look to keep up with the Joneses as opposed to doing the things they want to do for themselves and their families. If they are unable to succeed in impressing others, they will become increasingly desperate to portray themselves as successful.

Let's take a look at the unhealthy levels, that is, levels 7 to 9.

In **level 7**, Achievers are driven by their fear of failure. They are overly concerned about losing facing and being seen as worthless. So, they may resort to exploitation and manipulation to get their way.

Level 8 Achievers can become devious, deceptive and malicious to get their way. They will stop at nothing to achieve what they believe are to be their goals.

For **level 9** Achievers, vengeance becomes their main drive. They will strive to get back at those people whom they blame for their failures. If they believe their parents are at fault for their failures, they will do everything they can to punish their parents for keeping them from achieving their goals.

The biggest potential addiction for Type Threes is workaholism. They may also resort to abuse of stimulants to help them keep up with their pace. They may also become overly concerned with their outward image as beauty may become very important to them.

Here are some recommendations for Type Threes in their development journey.

- It is important to keep true to yourself. You need to be in touch with your feelings so that you understand what is driving you. When you understand what is driving you, you will be able to make sense of the negative feelings that may be spurring you on.

- Fostering positive relationships is important. If you are focused on helping others grow alongside you, you will become a positive influence on everyone around you.

- Focusing on goals and projects which will benefit you and your community is essential. Type Threes can fall into a trap in which they take on too much. They have a hard time saying "no". So, it is important to keep this in mind.

- Being generous with your time and efforts is a great way of finding balance. So, if you are keen on achieving what you want, but also helping others achieve their own goals, you will be able to balance your feelings of personal development and the sense of worth in the greater community.

Type threes make great leaders. At their best, they can be influential folks who motivate others to be the best they can become.

Chapter 5

Type Four: The Individualist/Performer

In this chapter, we are going to be taking a look at the personality type corresponding to the Individualist or Performer. We will also be referring to this personality type as Type Four as per the order we are following.

The Individualist can be perceived as a negative trait on the surface. This stems from the fact that the Individualist is more apt to be introspective, that is, more in tune with themselves rather than being more outward and expressive. One might consider that the Individualist is the opposite of the Helper in the sense that the Helper is focused solely on others whereas the Individualist is more inclined toward focusing on themselves.

This is an important distinction to take into consideration as most folks may misinterpret the individualist's nature as being self-absorbed. And while this is true in the lower levels of development, the fact of the matter is that the Individualist is capable of great sensitivity and care so long as they are provided the opportunity to act on their own without pressure from external sources.

It is also worth mentioning that this personality type is very keen on self-development and improvement. However, this individual is more inclined to their personal development as opposed to the Reformer who is more inclined in making changes across the board. This is what gives the Individualist a great deal of sensitivity and appreciation for the finer points in life. They are very appreciative of the minutiae in life which tends to go unnoticed by most folks.

The most significant fear for Type Fours is having a lack of self-identity. As such, Type Fours are the kind of folks who are constantly looking to find themselves. These are individuals who are prone to do soul-searching regularly. When they can conquer these fears, they can come to grips with who they are and what they stand for. When they can find their self-identity, they become exceptional in whatever their choose field is.

Hence, Type Fours' biggest wish is to find out who they are. Don't be surprised if you know individuals who spend most of their early adult years traveling the world, or bouncing around from job to job until they finally settle into one chosen profession. Superficially, many folks will accuse them of lacking discipline and focus. However, on a deeper level, all they are doing is looking to find what they wish to achieve out of life.

The biggest driving force behind Individualists is their desire to express themselves, that is, their creativity and individuality. This is what makes them great artists and performers. That is why the second word used to describe this personality type is "performer". Please bear in mind that these are folks who thrive in artistic fields, or sports, in which individual performance is the key. They may not excel in team sports unless they have the opportunity to stand out individually. For example, team sports such as Rugby in which one individual cannot dictate the pace of the game may not be the most suited for this personality type. However, sports such as basketball, in which one individual can be the difference-maker, can be good options for this personality type.

Also, artistic fields in which they are left to their own devices can suit Type Fours very well. While they may thrive in more collaborative efforts, they will be at their best when they can express themselves to the fullest. When you think of Type Fours, think of folks such as Criss Angel, Bob Dylan, Frida Kahlo, and Tennessee Williams. These are artists and performers who have stood out based on their merits. Their legacy is based on their talents as opposed to more collaborative efforts.

A balanced Type Four will accept every facet of themselves. They will embrace the good with the bad. They will accept their virtues as well as their flaws. As such, they won't be intimidated by having to deal with situations and circumstances outside of their comfort zone so long as they feel they can learn something about themselves.

Individualists on the lower end of the self-development scale may become withdrawn and unavailable to most folks. They have trouble socializing and developing meaningful relationships. Often, they may have trouble finding romantic partners and keeping a healthy social life. In extreme cases, some individuals become hermits and close themselves off to the world around them.

It should be noted that Individualists don't seek to be alone. Rather, they place a high value on meaningful relationships. Hence, they are very picky when it comes to the people with whom they socialize. Therefore, if a person does not meet their standards, they will generally refrain from engaging people that won't contribute to their development and growth. One telltale sign of this personality type is a person who says they would rather spend one on one time with a close friend rather than going to a loud party filled with people.

Now, let's take a look at the various levels of development for Type Fours. First, let's look at levels 1 to 3 which are considered to be the healthy levels.

In **level 1**, Individualists are deeply creative and inspired. They value their self-image and seek to portray that outward as an expression of their creativity. They are sensitive individuals who value people and relationships greatly.

Level 2 Individualists are very introspective and find themselves on a continuous search for themselves. They are keen to express themselves through the various artistic means available to them.

A **level 3** Individualist is true to themselves. You may find them living up to code, or standard, that is a reflection of their individuality. They can be shy or withdrawn at times though they have no trouble communicating with others. They can be very kind and helpful so long as they are not overburdened by interactions with others.

The next levels, 4 to 6 refer to average levels of development for the Type Four personality.

A **level 4** Individualist will come off as artistic and creative. They embrace the beauty of life. However, they may live in a fantasy world and become prone to daydreaming more than usual.

In **level 5**, an Individualist will be very much in tune with their feelings and creative nature. Nevertheless, their shy and withdrawn personality may come more into focus. They will be less inclined to partake in social activities shying away from interactions with other folks. While these are hardly socially challenged individuals, they may not be as sociable as the folks in the higher levels of development. As such, they may exhibit signs of withdrawal and unavailability.

Level 6 Individualists will show themselves to be very different from "regular" folks. They may sink themselves into overly melancholic dreams. They may even become detached from the real world to live in a dreamland that they have created for themselves. While these folks are hardly schizophrenic, they tend to lose touch with reality. This leads them to become self-indulgent and often unproductive.

Now, let's take a look at the lower, or unhealthy, levels for Individualists.

In **level 7**, an Individualist may become angry and alienated from the real world. They may claim that no one "gets them". This can be used to justify their lack of social skills and interaction with others. This can lead to feelings of shame and cause withdrawal.

Level 8 Individualists live in torment. They often blame others for their failure to make anything of themselves. They tend to harbor feelings of self-contempt and self-loathing. They may even have thoughts of harming themselves.

Finally, **a level 9** Individualist may end up engaging in self-destructive behavior such as excessive drinking and substance abuse. They will consume anything to help them escape the reality which they face to embrace an alternate reality they wish to create for themselves. These individuals are narcissistic and may even attempt to take their own life.

The biggest plight of this personality type is self-indulgence. This can be seen in a lack of self-control and abuse of food, alcohol, and drugs. They may show signs of narcissism and excessive concern for outer appearance.

Here are some useful tips to get over some of the tougher aspects Type Fours may have to face.

- Monitor your feelings in such a way that you do not allow them to ruin your life. Of course, it is important to worry about the way others perceive you. However, it is important to make sure that this doesn't ruin your life. You are far more than your outward appearance conveys.

- Finding your mission, or purpose, in life will give you a sense of belonging. This will help you to stay productive and contribute to society in a meaningful way.

- To keep your self- esteem and self-confidence running high, try to make the most of every opportunity you have to experience positive results. When you can take positive experiences and build on them, you will be able to make the most of life's opportunities.

- Self-discipline is important. You can build your self-discipline through consistent routines such as regular bedtime and exercise regimen.

- Try your best to put your imagination and creativity to the service of others. For example, you can contribute your artistic talents for the enjoyment of others in addition to your remunerated endeavors. Make a point of providing joy to others through your talents.

Type Fours are certainly the most creative bunch in this entire list of personality types. At their best, they can stand out as some of the most inspiring individuals you will ever meet.

Chapter 6

Type Five: The Investigator/Observer

In this chapter, we are going to be taking a closer look at the Investigator personality type. This is also known as the "Observer". We will also be referring to this personality type as Type Five throughout this chapter.

The Investigator is a highly intellectual personality type that is focused on rationalizing things. The more they can make sense about the things inside them and around them, the easier it is for them to get along with the world.

At their best, Type Fives are very capable individuals who can find answers to some of the most complex issues. If you happen to know a healthy Type Five, they will thrive on the challenge of finding answers to issues that perhaps no one else has been able to find. They are very curious, inquisitive and cerebral.

The biggest downside to the Investigator personality type is that they may become detached of their feelings in favor of a rational approach. As such, they may lack the ability to connect with other folks on a deeper, more emotional level. They may even become emotionally unavailable when they are unable to find answers or make sense of things.

The main driving force pushing Type Fives is their desire to be seen as capable and competent. These are the folks that place a high degree of value on college degrees, honors and academic

38

recognition. In the professional world, they may place a great deal of value on awards. For instance, sports stars will measure their overall value on being champions and getting awards. Often, Investigators in athletics can advance the science of a sport.

The underlying fear of Type Fives is being seen as unintelligent or incompetent. An Investigator may fall into a deep depression if they are unable to succeed in academics or if they get stumped in solving an issue. They may also become obsessed with find the answer to a problem until they find the solution to it.

Some of the most notable Investigator types are: professor Stephen Hawking, pianist Glenn Gould, Microsoft founder Bill Gates and film director Alfred Hitchcock. These folks are luminaries in their respective fields. While they all come from different backgrounds, they all challenged the limits of their chosen fields. They were able to make breakthroughs or achieve outcomes which many had thought impossible to achieve. In particular, Stephen Hawking was considered to be the most intelligent person during his lifetime.

Type Fives are known as Investigators due to their inquisitive nature. They take learning very seriously. To them, the main purpose in life is to be on a constant path to learning. This is something highly positive as it allows for greater introspection. This can lead Type Fives to learn so much about themselves. This is why they are often seen as very mature individuals.

Investigators are also known for their penchant for reflection and daydreaming. Of course, this nature is what enables them to come up with breakthroughs that many of them achieve. Even if their innovations are related to their personal life, they can make dreams happen.

On the flipside, this dreamy nature can lead them to lose touch with reality. When this happens, they may not fully appreciate the world around them. In the worst of cases, their inability to find answers to the questions that take up their attention may lead to frustration, and even depression, since they are unable to figure out why things are the way they are. Therefore, acceptance is one of the biggest challenges for Type Fives.

Perhaps on the biggest strengths of the Investigator personality type is that they don't depend on social validation. They don't need to be told they are smart and competent; they already know it. However, insecurity may take hold of them at some point. When this happens, they may seek validation in terms of awards and recognition. If this validation does not come, they may descend into an anxious state.

Let's take a deeper look at the Investigator type by their levels of personal development.

Levels 1 to 3 correspond to the levels of healthy development.

In **level 1**, the Investigator type is at its best. They are visionary and gain a profound comprehension of the way the world works. They can make the most of the situations around them. They are open-minded and deeply embrace change. They are true pioneers in their respective fields.

Level 2 Investigators are highly perceptive. Their deliver insights that ordinary individuals may not be able to provide. They are constantly searching for knowledge often finding value in their original contributions. They may also be considered quirky at times.

For a **level 3** Investigator, they are prone to achieve full mastery of their chosen field or craft. They can become experts in their respective areas of expertise. The produce original contributions which further the betterment of their communities, and why not, the world.

Next, we will see the average levels of development for Type Fives.

In **fourth level** of development, Type Fives will often find themselves working things out well in advanced before actually engaging in any kind of activity. They need to think things through before they commit to their actions. As such, they tend to overthink things.

In **level 5**, Investigators may begin to detach themselves from the world around them in favor of imaginary worlds. This is generally a response to their dissatisfaction with their reality. Instead of facing a reality that may not be what they expected, they fabricate imaginary circumstances. This may lead them to be perceived as delusional.

A **level 6** Investigator may take on an antagonistic posture against everything that does not mesh with their view of the world. Under these circumstances, Investigators may feel compelled to rebel against the system though not for the sake of positive change but for the sake of being right.

Levels 7 to 9 are considered unhealthy levels for Type Fives. They may exhibit some of the following traits.

In **level 7**, Investigators become isolated and nihilistic. Their detachment from reality becomes even more apparent. They are aggressive and will generally reject anything that they feel does not correlate to their visions of the world. They do not get along well in social settings.

Level 8 Investigators are obsessed with imposing their ideas on the world. They may even begin to show signs of delusional and paranoid behavior. While they are not at a point of mental illness, they are firmly detached from reality. They may become reclusive and completely isolated from the world around them.

Level 9 Investigators may have full-blown mental illness, dementia and even engage in self-destructive behavior. These individuals may seek to take revenge on the world and cause great harm. They would rather destroy the world rather than conform to societal expectations that don't adhere to their perceived version of the world. They would rather take their own lives as opposed to accepting their lack of worth in society.

Those Observers who succumb to addictions may find themselves neglecting their wellbeing such as hygiene, exercise and a balanced diet. They might make use of recreational drugs a habit as means of escaping reality. Otherwise, alcoholism may become an alternative escape.

Here are some tips and ideas which can help Type Fives navigate the waters of the world around them.

- It is important to recognize when you are overthinking things. Sometimes, a healthy balance between reason and intuition can help you make sense of the world. Also, recognizing your unique talents will help you identify your value to society.
- It is also important to take the time to relax and make the most of enjoying life. Being too intense and high-strung for

prolonged periods can lead to physical and emotional burnout.

- Also, try to avoid becoming judgmental. It is easy to denounce anything that doesn't conform with your views of the world. Hence, tolerance is an essential part of being balanced and healthy.

- Furthermore, try to address trust issues that you may develop as a result of being "disappointed" by others. When you feel that others don't follow in your lead, you may feel withdrawn and misunderstood. While there is nothing wrong with feeling out of place at times, there are circumstances in which you may need to be more flexible and tolerant with the situation around you.

Investigators are true visionaries. If you identify with this personality type, then take the time to make your dreams a reality. Find the best way to make you dreams come true.

Chapter 7

Type Six: The Loyalist/Skeptic

In this chapter, we are going to be taking a deeper look at the Loyalist personality type. This type is also referred to as the Skeptic. Furthermore, we are going to refer to this type as Type Six, therefore, the course of this chapter.

The Loyalist personality type can be seen at the "rock". These are highly dependable individuals in which you can count on at all times. That is why reliability is their strong suit. They are committed and disciplined in such a way that they see things through from beginning to end. When you identify with this personality type, you are not the kind that starts off a million things and doesn't see anything through to the end. It is quite the opposite. You are committed to seeing things as the last consequence.

In general terms, Type Sixes are great people to have around. You know they won't flake out on you at the last minute. When they give you their word, you can take that to the bank. However, they do tend to become indecisive when they are not at their best. They also tend to become defensive and evasive when they are not feeling comfortable in a situation. The worst thing that can happen to a Loyalist is to be backed into a corner. If this should happen, they may act out in a rebellious and defiant manner.

The most important driving force behind Type Sixes is security, stability, and support. They seek to have a stable environment at all times. If they lack a stable foundation, they will become overly anxious. This can lead them to feel unprotected. Hence, their biggest fear is to feel adrift, that is, floating through life without a sense of direction.

It should also be noted that the Loyalist type has no problem with following orders. They will recognize their place in the chain of command and roll with the punches. However, they will lash out if the official leadership does not provide the guidelines they are supposed to provide. While Loyalists have no trouble taking charge, they need to have guidelines and direction as much as possible.

Some notable Type Sixes include actor Robert DeNiro, former President Richard Nixon, film director Michael Moore, and philosopher Krishnamurti.

These notable figures all encompass the Loyalist nature, that is, they provide stability to those around them. In particular, former President Richard Nixon presided over one of the most difficult periods of American history. And while he stands as the only US President to have resigned, he is remembered for having taken some of the most difficult decisions in history.

The folks who are identified as a Type Six receive the moniker as the "Loyalist" for good reason. In addition to being the most dependable type in the Enneagram of Personality, these folks are the most loyal to their friends, family, and beliefs. These individuals are the last to turn their back on what they believe in and the people they love. As such, they are incredibly reliable even in the harshest of circumstances.

However, as much as they can serve as the rock of their social group, they also need to know that they have the support of those around them. If you have close to a Type Six, then you need to serve them as a source of support from which they can draw strength. Despite the resolve, Type Sixes are not lone wolves. So, they need to know that someone has got their back as much as they've got others' backs.

Given the fact that the underlying fear of the Loyalist is finding themselves with a lack of support, they may end up lacking self-confidence. This will lead them to doubt their own ability to guide and lead the way. Now, this is not to say that they are not good leaders, but if left alone, self-doubt can creep in and undermine their confidence in their ideas and decisions. This is why they are also known as "skeptics" since self-doubt is an issue Type Sixes must deal with throughout their lives.

When perfectly balanced and healthy, Loyalists will have rock-solid faith in their ideas and decisions. At their worst, they might be unable to function without being led. Thus, they will need constant guidance and support. They may doubt their abilities to a point where they might not be able to fully function independently.

Now, let's take a look at the various personal development levels for the Type Six personality type.

First off, levels 1 to 3 are balanced and health levels.

In **level 1**, the Loyalist type is perfectly independent, self-reliant and able to take charge when needed. They are cooperative and highly dependable. They can become cornerstones of any group, team or institution. They make great leaders and hold to their relationships and convictions.

For **level 2** Loyalists, trust is the foundation of their relationships. They can bond with others, foster cooperative relationships and make solid partnerships. They can elicit the best possible performance from others around them.

Level 3 Loyalists are dedicated to their communities, companies, and families. They are responsible, hardworking and trustworthy. People around them value the stability they bring to the table. They make excellent managers and captains.

Now, let's look at the average levels of development, that is, levels 4 to 6.

In **level 4**, the Loyalist type is reliable and trustworthy. They are good at following authority and can be relied upon to the job done when needed. They need structure and guidance to flourish.

For a **level 5** Loyalist, self-doubt may creep in. They may become anxious and evasive as they try to avoid taking on greater responsibility. They may be prone to procrastination and ambivalence. They need a strong support network to fully realize their potential.

A **level 6** Loyalist may be rather insecure. They may choose to act out and rebel as a means of coping with their insecurities. They may also seek to blame others for their lack of security. If put into a leadership role, they may prove to be authoritarian while showing signs of suspicion, paranoia, and insecurity at a deep level.

Levels 7 to 9 are considered the unhealthy levels for a Type Sixes.

In **level 7**, a Type Six might live in constant fear of having their insecurities exposed. They may easily panic and show their signs of inferiority. They might end up feeling defenseless and may depend considerably on those around them.

Level 8 Loyalists may have feelings of persecution, that is, that someone is out to get them. They may resort to violent behavior to assert themselves in their social circle.

For a **level 9** Loyalist, hysteria may take over. They may have to resort to alcoholism, drug abuse of any other type of substance abuse to cope with their fears and insecurities. These individuals may be unable to fully function in the real world. They may become co-dependent on a parent or spouse. Suicidal tendencies are not out of the questions.

Type Sixes are prone to substance abuse when going through a difficult time. They may also engage in workaholism especially if they become an indispensable member of an organization. They may also resort to caffeine and other stimulants to keep them going through addiction to antidepressants may prove to be evident as well.

Based on the personal development levels, here are some general guidelines which can help Type Sixes fully grow and develop.

- Managing anxiety is key. That is why understanding the root of your anxiety is important to get a grip on it. Please remember that you are not alone. If you feel that there is no one out there for you, then you need to seek help from professionals who can aid you when needed.

- Self-doubt is also a persistent issue. If you feel that you begin to question yourself or the decisions you have made, bear in mind that you have succeeded even more times than you have failed. Your successes are all the evidence you need to prove that your instincts and judgment are right. It is also important to avoid letting others plant a seed of doubt in your mind.

- Stress management is also an important factor to keep in mind. If you don't get a handle on stress, it can undermine your ability to keep a level head when having to act under duress. Relying on your support network in times of difficulty can become a true lifesaver.

- Thus, developing a strong support network will help you get the grounding you need to keep you from going off course.

Type Sixes are highly dependable individuals who will serve as the cornerstone of a family or organization. If you identify with this personality type, please keep in mind that you don't have to do everything on your own. There are others to support you.

Chapter 8

Type Seven: The Enthusiast/Epicurist

In this chapter, we are going to delve into the personality type known as the "Enthusiast". This type can also be referred to as the "Epicurist". Throughout this chapter, we are going to refer to this type as "Type Seven", as well.

The Enthusiast type in the Enneagram is, by far, the most extroverted and happy-go-lucky type. These are playful, cheerful and simply fun people to be around. They are the life of the party. They are the kind of individuals who can lighten the mood especially if things are tense. Type Sevens should not be confused with "class clowns" since these so-called clowns tend to be folks with low self-esteem that don't mind being the butt of others' jokes.

On the flip side, the Enthusiast type may be considered to be undisciplined and unruly. In the worst of cases, these are individuals who lack direction and purpose. One might consider them to be the opposite of the Loyalist personality type. Nevertheless, they can always be relied upon to crack a joke when most needed.

The fundamental driving force behind the Enthusiast type if they desire to have their needs fulfilled. This may be seen as an entitled nature. In reality, they seek their happiness and pleasure, hence the "Epicurist" tag. They will strive, as much as possible, to have their needs met with the least amount of effort possible. This is why their biggest fear and concern is to deal with pain and deprivation. Thus, they are light on tolerance and steadfastness.

The quintessential Type Seven is actor Jim Carrey. Other notable Type Seven includes legendary composer Mozart, business tycoon Richard Branson, and Academy Award Winner Robin Williams. These individuals all encompass the happy nature of this personality type. Mozart is renowned for having a lighthearted nature despite exploring very serious themes in some of his works. Richard Branson in an ultra-successful businessman who loves to have fun. Robin Williams though is a great example of how much a wonderful and magical person can succumb to the darkest side of this personality type.

In general terms, Type Sevens will light up a room. They are the most lovable and easygoing folks you will ever meet. They are highly sociable and have no trouble making friends, forming strong relationships and getting along well with others in cooperative situations. In the business world, they make great salespeople, public relations agents and some of the most beloved politicians.

On the flip side, their aversion to pain and sacrifice leads most observers to consider them weak and entitled. However, the fact of the matter is that they are not naturally averse to pain and sacrifice. If anything, they will seek to find an easier and better way of doing things. Thus, they will try to avoid grinding along if there is an alternative. For instance, they would much rather drive if they can avoid walking. After all, driving takes less time than walking.

When Type Sevens get the proper support and guidance from those around them, they will have no trouble taking charge and become a positive influence on those around them. When left unsupported, they may resort to a life of pleasures. As such, they may end up "partying" too much or simply avoiding responsibility at all costs.

One common method that Type Sevens engage in is "trial and error", that is, they will seek out various careers, fields of study or disciplines until they find the right one for them. This is often seen as a lack of direction. That is why proper guidance, especially for younger Type Sevens, will help them find their ideal path.

Now, let's take a look at Type Sevens in the various levels of personal development.

Firstly, let's analyze levels 1 to 3, that is, the healthy levels.

In **level 1**, Enthusiasts will have a contagious attitude for life. They are highly positive folks who are awed and inspired by even the simplest things in life. They have a noble spirit that makes everyone happier. They tend to be highly spiritual.

For **level 2** Enthusiast, extroversion is the name of the game. They are very excitable individuals who are lively, cheerful and spontaneous. They light up a room when they enter. They can also be resilient and show great motivation.

Level 3 Enthusiasts are accomplished individuals who rise to the top of their respective fields. They showcase their talents and can often be seen revolutionizing their area of expertise as they search for better ways of doing things.

Let's take a close look at the average levels of personal development, that is, levels 4 to 6.

In **level 4**, the Enthusiast personality type can be seen as a restless individual who is constantly seeking to explore the world around them. They relish in jobs and occupations that won't keep them tied to a desk or an office. They love going out to see the world even if it means taking on more risk than most folks would care for. They are the ones who test the boundaries of the world.

Level 5 Enthusiasts tend to be hyperactive. They just can't seem to settle down. They have a hard time taking "no" for an answer but not always in a good way. They tend to find themselves always doing something even if it is not the most productive thing they could be doing with their time and energy. They may take on too many things at once and end up achieving very little.

A **level 6** Enthusiast will be prone to excess. This may come in the form of excessive greed and materialism. They may become consumed with the idea of looking good, living in luxury and having a lavish lifestyle. They may become pushy and demanding. They will expect others to comfort to their whims.

Levels 7 to 9 correspond to the unhealthy levels for the Enthusiast personality type.

In **level 7**, the Enthusiast may show themselves to be overly anxious. They may also have a hard time controlling their impulses. As such, they may engage in impulse shopping or resorting to addictions to quell their hyperactive nature. Drugs such as marijuana help calm their nerves and anxiety.

Level 8 Enthusiasts are known for mood swings. While they may not be bipolar, they will have erratic changes in mood. This leads to unpredictability which can even offend people. Their impulsive nature can lead to a lack of self-control which can land them in serious trouble.

The **level 9** Enthusiast is at wits end. This individual may have consumed their energy and good spirits. As such, they are completely spent. They may become paranoid, claustrophobic and rely heavily on drugs to keep them going. They may find themselves in deep despair, depression and lash out in self-destructive behavior. Suicide can be a consequence of this level. Bipolar disorder and borderline personality disorder may be issues as well.

In general, Type Sevens struggle with addiction, particularly drug abuse, or any type of stimulant. Also, their hyperactive nature can lead them to burnout. As such, they may become dependent on painkillers and other types of opiates.

Here are some useful tips and strategies which can help Type Sevens stay at their best.

- Self-control is vital. Recognizing when you are feeling impulsive is a great way to find a good balance. If you feel that you are losing control, you can take a step back. That way, you won't act on your impulses leading you to potentially irrational behavior.
- Also, putting others ahead of yourself is a great way in which you can foster strong relationships with those around you.
- Embracing silence and solitude are also great ways of balancing out your social and extroverted nature. Downtime is essential to replenish energy and strength.
- Furthermore, being aware of the quality of your interactions in life will help you to focus on what matters. For example, it is best to have a small group of real friends as opposed to

having a large social circle that is not conducive to meaningful relationships.

- Try to remain focused on what you want out of life. It is easy to bounce around from one place to another. In the long run, however, this unpredictable nature can lead to a lack of direction and structure.

At their best, Type Sevens are wonderful and magical people to be around. They can become the type of person we all aspire to be. That is why honing in on talents and skills can help Type Sevens find the direction they seek.

Chapter 9

Type Eight: The Challenger/Protector

In this chapter, we are going to be taking a look at the eight-personality type of the Enneagram called the "Challenger". This personality type is also referred to as the "Protector". Throughout this chapter, we will be referring to it as Type Eight.

The Protector personality Type is a very strong type by definition. This is the strongest type in the Enneagram as the folks who identify with the personality are geared toward taking care of others. The kind of protection that they provide can be physical, emotional, or perhaps both. They are the quintessential keepers. They are in tune with controlling their environment. As such, they are not afraid of responsibility. These individuals tend to act as heroes and champions.

At its best, the Protector is an individual who will not back down from a fight. They are glorious and often assertive. Their main driving force is to be in control of their destiny. They hate depending on others. They would much rather face incredible odds than lose control.

On the flipside, they can be aggressive and intimidating. They can attack those around them when they don't get their way. They can degrade into bullies. At their worst, they are domineering and egocentric. Needless to say, this is not the noblest side of the Protector.

As a result, the Protector's biggest underlying fear is being hurt and/or losing control. At times, they can be emotionally unavailable as they are afraid of letting others get too close to them. However, this fear can be offset by setting up a system in which they have control of everything that goes on around them. Indeed, the Protector is a control freak.

That is why the main driving force behind the Protector is to be completely independent and self-reliant. They have no trouble working long hours, bearing tough situations or dealing with harsh conditions so long as they have the chance to choose their fate.

Some notable Protectors include humanitarian Oskar Schindler, writer Ernest Hemingway, and United States President Donald Trump. All of these individuals have a steadfast nature in common. They were not afraid to back down from a challenge. Ernest Hemingway worked his way up from being a beat reporter for small-town newspapers to become one of the greatest writers in the history of literature. Oskar Schindler risked his life to save hundreds of Jews from Nazi persecution during World War II. Ultimately, Schindler had to flee to save himself from the Nazis. US President Donald Trump has proven to be steadfast in the face of tremendous opposition from all angles. He is a great example of how the Protector is not afraid of fights to defend what they believe to be right.

It should be noted that the main reference to this personality type is the Challenger since the folks who identify under this description are not afraid of putting up a fight. They will not back down until they have been defeated. And even then, don't be surprised if they come back. After all, what doesn't kill them only makes them stronger.

However, this steadfast nature can quickly degrade into stubbornness. This is important to keep in mind as successful Challengers need to strike a balance between being strong and steadfast while knowing when to back down. As such, there is a fine line between showing no fear and being foolhardy. Often, the Challenger type can take on a fight that is too big for them. Consequently, their defeats can crush their spirit. If such a case were to occur, the Challenger will come back with a chip on their shoulder. Yet, this attitude may lead them to act out of spite and not a sheer desire to help and/or protect others.

While the Protector, or Challenger, is one of the toughest individuals you will meet, they can quickly become overly aggressive, narcissistic and even turn into bullies. If they have a hard time getting a grip on their aggression, they will needlessly run over people who had no intention of harming them. When they are under large amounts of stress, they will lash out against those around them. This makes them very much unlikeable.

Nevertheless, they are pillars of strength from which other individuals can derive fortitude and solace when things are going tough. Challengers are the type of folks whom you can count on to have your back when you get into trouble.

Now, let's take a look at the various levels of development for the Challenger personality type.

The first levels, 1 to 3, pertain to the healthy levels.

In **level 1**, the Challenger type is very disciplined and restrained. They know they have great power and use it to protect others who are not as strong. They use their authority appropriately and courageously stand up for those who need a voice. They know when to back down. They may achieve tremendous exploits of heroism.

Level 2 Protectors are assertive and self-confident. They are, by no means, a pushover. They take initiative and leadership when the situation warrants it. They keep a can-do attitude at all times and will spare no effort to encourage others to get things done.

Level 3 Challengers are decisive, commanding and authoritative without degrading into pushing people around. They take the initiative when needed and raise their voice to champion people and causes that need their support.

Now, let's look at levels 4 to 6, which are considered to be average levels of personal development.

In **level 4**, the Challenger type is prone to self-sufficiency, independence and pragmatism. They don't need anyone to do anything for them. Even when they get into trouble, they don't need help or handouts. Consequently, it may be very hard for them to ask for help when they need it. Their strength may be confused with arrogance and pride.

Level 5 Protectors are control freaks. They need to dominate their environment to ensure that they have control over the situations which may arise. They are proud and often self-centered though not entirely selfish. They are very much interested in imposing their point of view on others.

Level 6 Challengers are feisty. They will challenger everything around them until they get their way. This early manifestation of stubbornness can sabotage their success. They have trouble respecting others' authority. Needless to say, they don't play well with other kids.

Now, let's have a look at the unhealthy levels for the Challenger personality type, that is, levels 7 to 9.

In **level 7**, a Protector may begin to degrade into a bully. They may be ruthless in their actions. They are swift to impart their brand of justice. You are basically with them, or against them. They may descend into a high degree of violence.

Level 8 Challengers may end up developing delusional ideas about their power and authority. They begin to have delusions of grandeur in which they may develop a dictatorial attitude. They believe they are the only ones who hold the right answers. They will spare no effort to get others to go along with them.

In **level 9**, Challengers may well have descended into full dictator mode. They will use violence and force to impose their will. They will not stop until everyone has submitted to their will. They need to be recognized as the supreme leader. These individuals may even be borderline schizophrenics.

Their main addictions lie in self-indulgence. Hence, they may battle with weight their entire lives. Also, they tend to manage high levels of stress. As such, they are prone to diseases such as high blood pressure, stroke and coronary issues. They may also engage in substance abuse.

Here are some key insights to help Protectors develop their abilities to the fullest.

- Self-discipline and restraint are important qualities. You need to recognize your power and how it should be used only to protect others from harm and injustice. Save your energies and focus on times when others need you.

- It is also important to learn how to yield every so often. You don't lose power and authority by admitting that others are right. Taking advice from others only reaffirms your self-confidence as it shows that you are not afraid of listening to others.

- Being self-reliant is a hallmark of this personality type. Yet, don't be afraid to ask for help when you need it. It doesn't make you any less of a champion to recognize that there is something which you cannot do alone. Asking for help will only make others see you as someone flexible as opposed to stubborn.

- Also, try to avoid placing too much emphasis on holding power and control. While it is fundamental for Type Eights to have power and control, do not allow this to cloud your judgment. If anything, delegating authority to others will help you sleep a lot better at night.

When balanced, Type Eights are the ultimate protectors and champions. If you have such a person in your life, you will never vulnerable and unprotected.

Chapter 10

Type Nine: The Peacemaker/Mediator

In this chapter, we are going to be taking a look at the final personality type in the Enneagram. This personality type is the "Peacemaker" which is also known as the "Mediator". Besides, this personality type will be referred to as Type Nine throughout this chapter.

As its name suggests, the Peacemaker is all about finding a happy medium whenever there is the potential for conflict. In many ways, the Peacemaker is the direct opposite of the Challenger. As such, the Peacemaker's goal is to avoid conflict as much as possible. Their main aim is to achieve harmony and togetherness.

Perhaps the biggest misconception is that the Peacemaker is a pushover. That is hardly the case when Type Nines find themselves in balance. A solid and healthy Type Nine will be firm in the posture but will always try their best to find common ground that leads to a win-win for all of those involved.

In general terms, the Peacemaker is easygoing and receptive. At their best, they a very "zen", that is, they hold a great deal of inner peace. As such, they are not at war with themselves. Rather, they know who they are and what they are capable of achieving. This is a feeling of peace that they transmit to their fellows. They are great teammates and colleagues.

When they are not at their best, Type Nines can descend into feelings of loss and desperation. They may feel out of place and shift to the opposite end of the spectrum by becoming jaded and mistrusting of others. Moreover, they may refuse to cooperate with others choosing aloofness and withdrawal.

The innermost element driving Type Nines is their desire for inner peace. Their search for stability and wholeness is what drives them to become who they are. Peacemakers are prone to accepting situations that they may not agree with but will do so out of their necessity for peace. In a way, they fell that if they acquiesce with what others won't, they can put conflict behind them.

On the other hand, a balanced and healthy Type Nine will be able to draw a line in the sand and make their voice heard. They will assert their position as they have no qualms about who they are and what they stand for. This is why a balanced Peacemaker is hardly a pushover.

However, Type Nines' biggest fear is loss. They fear losing their support network or mechanism. They would much rather acquiesce than lose their loved ones and friends. This is why peace is so valuable to them. Peacemakers feel that conflict will ultimately leave them all alone without their support network behind them.

Notable Type Nines include Princess Grace of Monaco, General Colin Powell, former President Ronald Reagan, and ex-Beatle Ringo Starr. An interesting example of these legendary individuals is Ronald Reagan who was at the helm when the Berlin Wall fell. He was instrumental in achieving peace by ending the Cold War, but at no time did he succumb to the pressures of the former Soviet

Union. He was able to stand his ground in defense of democracy around the world.

As mentioned earlier, the Peacemaker personality type is all about peace and harmony. They will also take on the role of mediator whenever possible. This is why the term "Mediator" has been tagged onto this personality type. Type Nines will do whatever they can to help others solve their issues and make the most of the opportunity they have to make peace.

Type Nines also tend to be very spiritual. They are generally in touch with their deeper selves. This is why their desire for peace is so profound. Hence, wholeness takes center stage when going about their life. In some of the more extreme cases, Type Nines may become hopeless romantics and idealists. They may dream of world peace in crisis and war.

On the flipside, Type Nines who lose touch with reality may become too overly optimistic. When reality clashes with their views of a peaceful and harmonious world, they may become jaded and resentful. This is especially true if they feel they have been unjustly wronged. This may, in turn, lead them to feel that they have been cheated.

When Type Nines descend into depression and despair, they may become completely pessimistic and dark. They may even try to numb out their pain through substance abuse or self-harm. In a way, they might feel as though they failed to achieve wholeness. Hence, they take their frustrations out on themselves. Thus, this leads to self-destructive behavior.

Now, let's take a look at the various levels of personal development for the Type Nine personality type.

First, let's have a look at the healthy levels, that is, levels 1 to 3.

In **level 1**, Peacemakers are fulfilled. They are filled with hope and are optimistic to the core. The fight for equality and justice. They will raise their voice for the causes they feel are just. Since they are at one with themselves, they will strive to have deep and meaningful relationships with those they choose to do so.

In **level 2**, Peacemakers are trusting and accepting. They are welcoming especially to those individuals who may have suffered from some type of exclusion of persecution. They are calm, serene and peaceful. The lack malice with themselves. They are simply good-natured people.

Level 3 Peacemakers are optimistic and reassuring. If you happen to have a counselor or therapist of this nature, you will find that they automatically help you feel at ease as soon as you saw them smile. They make great judges as they are impartial and fair, but genuine and caring.

Now, let's take a look at the average levels of personal development, that is, levels 4 to 6.

In **level 4**, a Peacemaker will act more out of fear of conflict that a genuine desire for peace. As such, they will strive to avoid conflict more than solve it. They are very complacent and may have a hard time asserting their position.

For **level 5** Peacemakers, conflict is their prime focus. They try as hard as they can to avoid becoming involved in a conflict. They may begin to withdraw and simply go with the flow. They may even begin to tune out when things begin to get rough.

Level 6 Peacemakers will do everything they can to avoid conflict altogether. They may even begin to shift to the opposite end of the spectrum by becoming increasingly pessimistic and stubborn. They feel that if they can't do anything to solve a conflict, then it's just best to stand by and watch the world burn.

Now, let's have a look at the unhealthy levels for this personality type, that is, levels 7 to 9.

In **level 7**, Peacemakers may feel incapable of dealing with conflict. Any type of issue will cause them to feel. They may even become neglectful of themselves and their duties. They may even start to become out of touch with their feelings.

For a **level 8** Peacemaker, dissociation may become the most effective coping mechanism for conflict. In a sense, they become someone else to get around the issues that bother them. They simply go through the motions when the going gets tough. Fear may get a grip on them.

Finally, a **level 9** Peacemaker may end up becoming a shell of who they once were. They may become completely oblivious to the reality around them. They may become paralyzed by fear and insecurity. They may even crumble completely in the face of adversity. Suicidal tendencies may be something to look out for at this stage.

Here are some tips and strategies which can help Peacemakers find the balance and wholeness they seek:

- Being assertive is fundamental to maintaining harmony. There is a point where you must draw the line to avoid others taking advantage of your agreeable nature.

- It is also important to stay in tune with what is going on around you. If you feel compelled to tune out when things are getting tough, then you might find that circumstances may end up becoming too overwhelming for you to deal with.

- If you find yourself in the middle of conflict, it would be wise to assess your role in the causing or diffusing it. If you find that you are causing the conflict rather than quelling it, then it might be time to take a deeper look at the role you are playing in that situation.

- Also, make sure that stays in tune with your body and your emotions. You need to stay in touch with the way you feel both physically and emotionally.

When at their best, Type Nines can be the comforting folks that you seek to have around you. They can be a soothing presence in the middle of turmoil.

Chapter 11

The Influence of Wings

In this chapter, we are going to be looking at "wings" and how they influence the core personality types of the Enneagram.

In the previous chapters, we took an in-depth look at the core personality types. As we have established, there are 9 core personality types. And while they all have some common elements among them, they are all different personality types.

However, it should be noted that there is no single person who is a pure core personality. What that means is that everyone has influences from other personality types. So, when reading the personality descriptors, if you felt that the descriptions from other personality types applied to you, then you might be getting close to figuring out your wings.

A good comparison of this is the Zodiac. Each Zodiac sign has pure characteristics attached to it. Nevertheless, no one is a pure Zodiac sign. They always influence a secondary sign. This secondary sign is what gives each individual their nuances when it comes to their personality and character.

As such, the same concept applies here. The core personality type that every one of us identifies with is influenced by its corresponding wing. As a result, it is important to understand what that wing is and how that applies to how our personality takes shape.

It should also be mentioned that our environment plays a key role in our overall behavior and personality. Since humans are in constant evolution, there is no denying that the circumstances in which we live in play a vital role in molding the way we handle ourselves. Nevertheless, our core personality remains the same throughout our lifetime.

Here is a good look at how the entire Enneagram of Personality is represented as a whole:

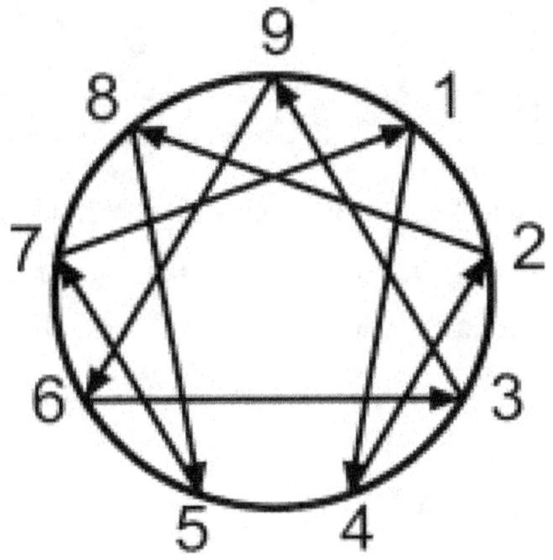

Source: Fitzel.ca

The diagram represents all 9 personality types in action. As you can see, they are all interrelated. Thus, they do not exist in isolation. Quite the opposite, they are all interconnected in one fashion or another. That is why there is a specific order to how we presented the personality types at the beginning of this book.

Once you have identified your core personality type, you can then look at the secondary characteristics which apply to you, that is, your wings. For instance, if you identify yourself as a Type One, then your wings will be Type Nine and Type Two. As such, the personality types adjacent to yours, to the left and the right, are your wings.

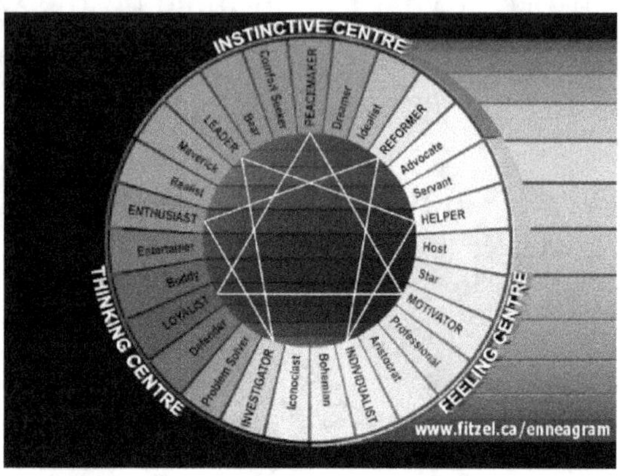

Thus, your wings represent a secondary influence on your core personality. Of course, it should be pointed out that there are no personality types that are better than others. They all have equally positive and negative traits. Consequently, your wings will not "improve" or "affect" your core personality. They are simply additional influences which you must take into account.

In general terms, it is believed that we can only influence one wing. Much like the Zodiac, there can only be one secondary core personality. However, some students of the Enneagram believe that it is possible to influence both wings. For this book, we will entertain the possibility of influencing both wings as experience has shown that both wings can play an influential role in shaping an individual's overall personality.

It is also important to consider that even if there is the influence of two wings, there will always be one "dominant" wing. In that regard, your Enneagram personality test will reveal which of the wings is more predominant.

As such, when you are looking into your core personality, it pays to read up on both wings, the one to the left and the one to the right, to see which of the characteristic may apply most to you. That is why it is a good idea to read up on all nine personality types. That way, you can get a good idea of how these influences may work out on you.

In some cases, some folks have stated that their second wing has developed over time. So, in their younger years, they had their core personality plus their predominant wing. But over time, these folks have indicated that the characteristics of their second wing have evolved. As a result, they feel a greater influence from their second wing. This is why we believe that there is the possibility of influence from the second wing though it is worth pointing out that the development of a second wing may be more the result of experience and maturity rather than an individual's inherent traits.

One other important aspect to consider is the fact that the core personality type and the wings of an individual may be to blend over time. Hence, older individuals may not exhibit the pure traits of their core personality, but rather, a morphed version of their core personality and its wings. Indeed, this is very much possible especially if the individual has been working hard to offset the more negative aspects of their core personality and hone in on the positive aspects of their core personality in addition to those of their wings.

At the end of the day, it is worth mentioning that this can be a conscious effort. What that implies is that you, as a conscious being, can work on and focus on the aspects of your personality which you wish to develop. By the same token, you can choose to let the more negative aspects take hold of you. Of course, there are times when folks need help. In such cases, professional help will certainly aid in getting an individual through a rough patch. Nevertheless, we can all make a concerted effort to improve our personality as we see fit.

Ultimately, your wings are just as influence. Your core personality is what defines the basic makeup of your personality and character. So, do take the time to determine your basic core personality type. That is the perfect starting point for your personal development.

Chapter 12

Integration and Disintegration Points

In this chapter, we are going to be taking a look at a very important part of the transition through the evolution, or perhaps devolution of an individual. As such, the integration and disintegration points provide an important map for reaching one's full potential.

In each of the descriptions for the nine core personalities, we laid out the progression through the various levels of personal development that a person can go through as they make their way across their life.

As such, it is important to understand what each level of personal development is in greater detail.

First of all, we indicated how there are "healthy", "average", and "unhealthy" levels for each core personality type. Each level corresponds to a progression in which the individual may be improving upon themselves thereby unlocking their core personality's best traits, or perhaps sinking into a downward spiral in which their core personality's negative traits come to the forefront.

Thus, it is important to gain a better understanding of how each of these levels can be conceptualized. Here is a breakdown of what each level represents.

Healthy levels:

- Level 1: This is the level associated with "liberation". In other words, the individual has unlocked their potential.
- Level 2: The level is liked to "psychological capacity" meaning that the person has achieved their best mental and spiritual level.
- Level 3: This level is called "social value", that is, this is the level where the individual is contributing the most to their social group and/or community.

Average levels:

- Level 4: In this level, there is an "imbalance of the social role" that the individual is meant to play. There might a lack of awareness regarding the role they are expected to play.
- Level 5: This is also known as the level of "interpersonal control". Hence, this is the level the governs relationships with others around the individual.
- Level 6: This level is referred to as the level of "overcompensation". As such, this level seeks to make up for the things which the individual may be lacking.

Unhealthy levels:

- Level 7: This level is commonly referred to as the level of "violation", this is, there is a breakdown occurring at some point.
- Level 8: This level pertains to "obsession and compulsion". This means that an individual at this level will have succumbed to addictions and fixations on the things they believe they are lacking or that they are missing.

- Level 9: The final level is referred to as the level of "pathological destructiveness". This is the point in which the individual is essentially in self-destruct mode.

Based on the initial assessment carried out to determine a person's core personality, light can be shed on their level of personal development. From there, the individual can determine if they are on a path of integration or a path of disintegration.

To illustrate this path, let's start at the extremes.

Let's suppose that you have taken your assessment and you have found yourself to be at level 1. This means that you are a perfectly integrated and healthy person. While everything may seem great, please bear in mind that there is always the possibility of a trend downward. There are any number of things which can cause you to spiral into a descent: the death of a loved one, the loss of a job, a tragic accident, virtually any major event can trigger a descent into a path of disintegration.

Now, let's go all the way to the other end of the spectrum. Let's consider someone who is deep into level 9 and essentially ready to take their own life. Since there is no further way down, the only way is up. And just like the previous example, there are any number of things that can trigger a reversal on to the path of integration. For example, the discovery of oneself, meeting a wonderfully positive person, or a spiritual awakening, among many other things, can trigger a reversal.

The main thing to keep in mind is that the path to integration, which is generally what we all seek, begins with a heightened sense of awareness. When you are aware of who you are, what you stand for, and your role in life, you can begin to gain a stronger foothold in life.

If you find yourself in the middle of the pack, then you have just as much chance to trend upward as you do downward. What that means is that it is up to you to figure out which way you want to go. The most important action which you can take, today, is to live in the present. The single-most powerful factor that gets people on a downward slope is hanging on the past. Likewise, fearing the future will keep you in a constant state of emotional disarray. Hence, the solution to finding yourself on a path of integration will take you through the present while leaving the past behind. As for the future, you can always deal with that when the time comes.

In general terms, the path to integration, that is growth, will look something like this: 1, 7, 5, 8, 2, 4, 1, 9, 3, 6, 9. What this means we must first move around the entire Enneagram before we can reach the ultimate level of integration. That is why there will be times when you may feel like you're a level 9 before you can reach level 1.

On the other hand, your path to disintegration, or stress, will look something like this: 1, 4, 2, 8, 5, 7, 1, 9, 6, 3, 9. Once again, you will have to bounce around the Enneagram before you can truly fall into the pits of level 9.

It should also be noted that these levels will manifest behaviors according to your core personality and your wings. So, please refer to the descriptions for each personality type so that you can get an idea about the types of feelings you will encounter as you transition through the various levels of the Enneagram.

One final note: please bear in mind that you will never have a smooth journey, that is, levels 1, 2, 3, 4 and so on. You first need to experience the various levels of both healthy and unhealthy behaviors before you can truly reach your desired goals for your personal development.

Chapter 13

Subtypes

In this chapter, we are going to be taking a look at what the subtype is in the Enneagram of Personality and how they interact with the various personality types. Also, we will be looking at a more specific understanding of how each of these subtypes can influence your core personality.

The subtypes found in the Enneagram of Personality are essentially related to three main areas that are associated with three essential human needs:

1. The need for self-preservation: this is how we respond to the threat that we perceive.
2. The need for social interaction: these are the networks that we create within our social groups and communities.
3. One on one: these are the personal connections that we make with individuals. This can also be seen as the need for intimacy and finding a mate.

These needs all happen at an instinctual level. What that means is that we are not always fully conscious of when these needs are apparent in us. We tend to fulfill these needs without really paying much attention to them. That is, we don't wake up one day and say, "I need to beef up my self-preservation skills".

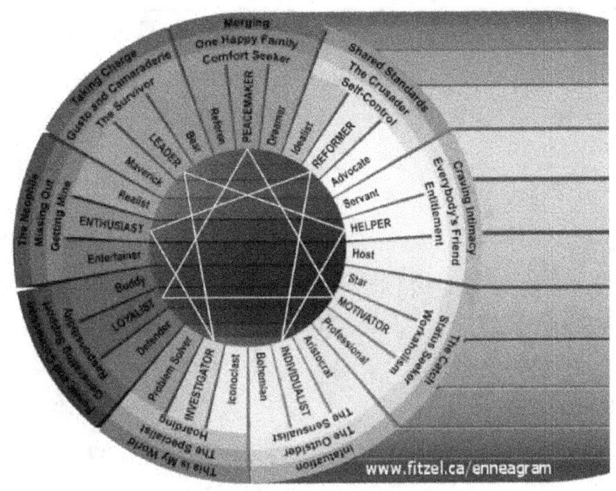

Since these needs are instinctual, they are present in every human being. Consequently, they make up part of our personality. Furthermore, they interact with our core personality type in such a way that it ultimately produces a specific behavioral pattern.

In all, there are 27 subtypes. Now, you might be thinking that's a lot. But it's just a numbers game. In essence, there are 3 instinctual subtypes and 9 core personality types. So, 3 multiplied by 9 equals 27.

With that in mind, let's take a look at how each of the 3 instinctual subtypes plays out with the 9 core personality types.

Instinctual Subtypes		
Self-preservation	**Social**	**One on one**
This subtype pertains to survival, which is physical security, shelter, food, and any resources needed to	This subtype pertains to the need for belonging and participation in broader social	This subtype deals with personal and intimate relationships, mating and the need for procreation. It

ensure personal survival and that of the family unit.	circles and communities.	can also extend to close friendships.
Type 1: this type is very much concerned about having order when it comes to all of the elements needed to ensure survival.	Type 1: If comfortable, this type has no problem fitting in. However, this type does not take change too well especially stepping out of their comfort zone.	Type 1: A possessive and jealous nature is not uncommon for this type. Nevertheless, they can be counted on to be dependable partners.
Type 2: While they are caring and nurturing, they may feel entitled to having their needs met.	Type 2: Approval and recognition are important to this type. However, they do value positive relationships over position.	Type 2: They may become demanding in terms of attention. Yet, they can form deep and meaningful bonds with their significant other.
Type 3: This type is concerned with gaining material possessions which can ensure security. They have the drive and energy to accomplish significant results.	Type 3: They are all about knowing the right people and getting "in". They are genuine leaders and can take on responsibility as needed.	Type 3: They have powerful charisma. However, they may be unsure about the true power of their sexuality. They are very concerned about their self-image.
Type 4: They are willing to move on	Type 4: This type is constantly looking	Type 4: This type may show feelings

to new situations if needed. They may even make reckless decisions without thinking them through.	for the best possible social role. However, they may become envious of those who achieve what they cannot.	of inadequacy. They generally value themselves with the power and strength of others. As such, this comparison may lead to their valuation to rise and fall as a result.
Type 5: This type views their home as their castle. They might tend toward hoarding resources in case of an emergency.	Type 5: They are concerned with attaining symbols of social status. They may even find themselves in a position where they cannot fully interact with others due to their tendency to overthink things.	Type 5: This type tends to have very personal and deep relationships. However, they will demand space and autonomy even in most intimate relationships.
Type 6: This type's biggest security threat is the loss of connection with their family or social network. This need takes precedence over material ones.	Type 6: They will play a role as a protector or guardian in this community. Knowing where they stand in their community will go a long way toward helping them feel comfortable and secure.	Type 6: This type can overcome their fears by showcasing their courage. This will help demonstrate their ability to create stability and maintain control in their lives and relationships.

Type 7: This type is very much concerned about having an abundant lifestyle. They cannot bear the idea of waiting for something.	Type 7: It might seem contradictory, but this personality type is very much willing to sacrifice themselves for the good of their social group.	Type 7: They are carefree and spontaneous. New ideas and adventures are what keep them going. They can easily get by on charm.
Type 8: This type is built for survival in a dog-eat-dog world. They are not afraid to put up a fight to ensure survival.	Type 8: They will take on a leadership role in which they can set a common agenda that ensures everyone's wellbeing.	Type 8: This type can be very possessive and dominant. They are willing to let go if need be. However, they may have a hard time giving their partner enough space and room to breathe.
Type 9: These folks are collectors. They will gather as many resources as they can though they are not hoarders. They will use up resources as needed to ensure their comforts.	Type 9: These are selfless leaders who are devoted to the common good of the group. However, they may lose sight of the group's overall priorities.	Type 9: This type yearns to be at one with their partner. Thus, this may cause issues with boundaries at times. Therefore, it is important to make sure that there are clear rules in the relationship.

The subtypes which we have described above are the result of general guidelines. As such, the influence of wings, as well as the environment, needs to be taken into account. Nevertheless, they provide a very good rule of thumb to take into consideration.

Chapter 14

Triads

In this chapter, we are going to be looking at a component of the Enneagram known as the "triads". The triads are three intrinsic elements that negatively affect core personalities. What his means is that they are rooted in unhealthy patterns.

The Enneagram of Personality is comprised of a fundamental element known as the triads. As the name suggests, these are three components that make up a negative influence upon the core personality types. Consequently, these negative influences can lead each of the personality types into a pattern of behavior which may cause the individual to go down the path of disintegration as opposed to the path of integration.

Also, it is important to consider that a fundamental understanding of the way triads work can lead the individual to gain deeper insight into these negative influences and how they can go about offsetting such influences. Hence, understanding what the triads represent provides folks with the opportunity to fully comprehend the nature in which they can maintain a healthy and balanced outlook on life.

Here are the triads:

1. The first triad is known as "fear". This is the "thinking" triad as it is associated with more intellectual and mental processes.

2. The second triad is known as the "anger" triad. This is the "instinctual" triad and it is associated with unconscious feelings or "gut" feelings as they can be referred to.
3. The third triad is the "shame" triad. This is a purely emotional triad and its influence can be linked to emotional reactions from an individual.

Under this concept, all of the negative feelings that a person has can be boiled down to any one of the triads, or a combination of two, or all three. The triads all represent emotions, feelings, and thoughts that a person has about the role they play in their social group, their self-image and how they perceive the world around them. For example, if an individual feels threatened at work, that is, they fear losing their job, the root feeling is fear, though the causes of this fear may vary significantly.

ANGER

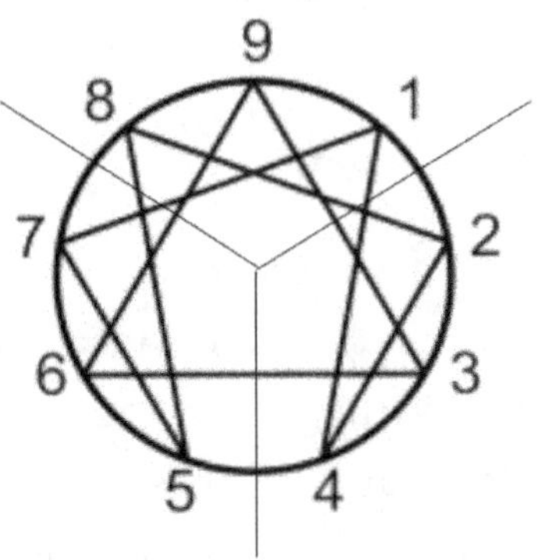

FEAR   SHAME

Adapted from: Fitzel.ca

As you can see in the image above, the triad cuts through the Enneagram in three equal parts. Therefore, anger is focused on 8, 9 and 1, shame on 2, 3 and 4 while fear is focused on 5, 6 and 7.

Besides, each one of these emotions has a specific action associated with it. For instance, anger is externalized, that is, it is projected outward. Likewise, shame is repressed or held in while fear and be internalized, that is, projected inward.

It is also important to note that each personality type hyper focuses on a specific part of the triad. What that means is that there is one specific emotion that tends to hit home more than the others. Here is what that looks like.

- Type 1: Internalizes anger.
- Type 2: Externalizes shame.
- Type 3: Represses shame.
- Type 4: Internalizes shame.
- Type 5: Externalizes fear.
- Type 6: Represses fear.
- Type 7: Internalizes fear.
- Type 8: Externalizes anger.
- Type 9: Represses anger.

Based on these reactions, you can cross-reference them to the core personality to see how that plays out in an individual's behavior. For example, Type Nine, the Peacemaker, will repress anger as much as possible. What that tells us is that a Type Nine, give the fact that they like to avoid conflict, will not express their anger outward. They will try to shove it way down to avoid an escalation in conflict.

Given this example, you can begin to link each one of these triads about the specific core personality. Now, it should be said that every core personality transitions through all of these emotions.

Yet, there is a specific hyper-focus on a single one of this triad. As such, you need to pay special attention to your core personality's hyper-focused emotion.

Consequently, let's take a look at some ways in which you can get a better grip on your hyper-focused emotions based on the triad.

- Type 1: This type tends to internalize anger, that is, focus in inward. Needless to say, this can become a dangerous and potentially self-destructive behavior as rather than lash out against other people or even the causes of their anger, they may lash out against themselves. As such, self-destructive behavior may lead to things such as addiction and substance abuse. That is why Type Ones need to find outlets for their feelings of anger, frustration and even guild.

- Type 2: This type tends to place shame outwardly, that is, on other folks. This can be seen by playing the "blame game". Consequently, Types Two need to avoid placing the blame on other people or making them feel bad when things don't go the way they expected. While taking responsibility for their actions is a great way to start, Type Twos should also focus on a collaborative effort in which placing responsibility squarely on one individual can be avoided.

- Type 3: This type's hyper-focus is to repress shame. What this means is that Type Threes will try to bury their feelings of guilt and inadequacy. While this may be effective for some time, these feelings will eventually come to the surface. When they do, they may leave the individual feeling emotionally distraught. This is why it is important to understand the source of these feelings and manage them accordingly. Often, counseling and having a support network can help alleviate these feelings before they even become an issue.

- Type 4: This type takes shame and focuses it on themselves. As such, they are prone to blaming themselves for the things that happen. This puts unnecessary pressure on themselves since not everything that happens in life is their fault. Of course, there is a need to take responsibility at times, but there is no need to bear the burden of everything that happens around them. Hence, it is important to be aware of these things which they can control and those which they cannot.

- Type 5: This type will project fear outward. This can come in the form of aggressive behavior. They may resort to intimidation and even certain levels of violence to get their way. That is why Type Fives need to avoid resorting to these tactics to get their way. It is often best to resort to dialogue to achieve a harmonious outcome.

- Type 6: This type is prone to swallow fear. Needless to say, this is not the healthiest of situations as shoving feelings way down only delays their ultimate effect. So, Type Sixes need to understand the source of their fears so that they can eventually face them and overcome them.

- Type 7: These types of projects fear inward. In the most extreme cases, this fear is enough to paralyze an individual and keep them from achieving anything in life. So, it is important to understand the root causes of fear and find adequate coping mechanisms for them. Often, having a support network is enough to help these types make their way through life.

- Type 8: This type tends to project their anger outward. Hence, the biggest challenge for this type is to exercise restraint and self-control. Naturally, uncontrolled outbursts can lead to irreparable consequences. Thus, exercising self-control becomes one of the most important things this type can do.

- Type 9: This type represses anger thereby become implosive. Over time, this implosive nature may lead to a serious emotional breakdown. Naturally, this is something that ought to be avoided at all costs. The main thing to keep in mind is that outlets are needed to vent pent up feelings. While there is no need for outbursts, there is the need for things such as exercise in which the individual can release the feelings they have been holding on to.

In general, a solid understanding of how the triads interact with your core personality will allow you to deal with these feelings more naturally. So, do take the time to go over the descriptions about how the triads affect your core personality and make a concerted effort to address these issues before they get the better of you.

Chapter 15

Determine Your Personality Type

In this chapter, we are going to be taking a deeper look at how you can go about determining your core personality type based on the model presented by the Enneagram of Personality.

Throughout this book, we have discussed the core personality types, the influence of wings and the triad. That is why further discussion is needed on how to determine your core personality type. In doing so, you will be able to establish your main characteristics and the influence that these have on the way you go about your life.

Now, it should be said that your core personality type is never expressed in pure form. In addition to the influence of your wings, there are environmental factors such as culture, socioeconomic status, religious beliefs and the circumstances that one must live through. All of these factors come into play when forging an individual's overall personality. Needless to say, there is no single factor that can perfectly mold a person's character.

Much like the Zodiac, the core personality type sets the foundation for a person's main traits though nothing is ever written in stone. When dealing with people, that is often the case. People are mutable and prone to change at any given moment especially when individuals make concerted efforts to improve upon or change aspects of their personality which they may wish to alter.

That being said, determine your personality type or that of those around you, is vitally important so that you can get the most out of the Enneagram model. At the outset of this book, we asked that you read through the descriptions of the nine personality types to get a feel for what they are like. Based on that, you could make an initial assessment as to which personality type fits in best with the way you perceive yourself.

Granted, that is not a foolproof method, but does allow you for an honest self-assessment. In doing so, it allows you to be honest with yourself and open the door for an exercise of introspection. Indeed, having the ability to be introspective enables you to become aware of the aspects which you feel you need to work on.

Naturally, there is a need for a more systematic and objective means of determining core personality types. As such, having a reliable means of testing is of the utmost importance. Of course, there are thousands of personality tests out there. There are some reputable and trustworthy tests such as the Myers-Biggs, which is essentially an industry standard, or less scientific tests like those found in the newspaper or the back of magazines.

Yet, all of these tests are ways in which you can find a more objective means of evaluating your personality type. This aims to take away any subjectivity that may come with making a personal assessment of one's personality.

In the case of the Enneagram, there are several types of tests out there. Earlier, we mentioned a couple of tests that are found on Enneagram websites. They are free and can be relied upon to provide you with a solid introduction to your core personality type.

Now, it should be pointed out that for most folks, a free test is enough to give them the spark they need to dig deeper into their personality. These free tests such as the one available at www.enneagramtest.com, can provide you with a great introduction into the nine core personality types. This test is a multiple-choice exam that you can do online. All you have to do is provide an email address in which your results will be sent to you. They do ask for donations after the results are provided, but that is entirely optional.

When you get your results, you will see a rather detailed description of that personality type. Once you have this core personality type, you can refer back to the Enneagram model and focus on your wings. So, if you are a Type One, then your wings will be 9 and 2. You would then need to look at their descriptions to gain a better sense of which of the wings is better suited to your personality.

As we mentioned in the section about wings, it is quite possible to influence both wings. While that is not entirely out of the question, it is more likely that you will have one predominant wing with a lesser influence from the other one. So, do take the time to go over both wings so that you can see where this influence might lie.

Another free option is the test offered by the Enneagram Academy. This test is a "light" version of the RHETI (more on that in a moment). This exam is much like the one offered by www.enneagramtest.com, and can be used to determine your core personality type. It consists of 36 multiple-choice questions. The results, while not scientifically validated, are rather accurate. So, it is certainly an option worth looking into.

The industry standard in terms of Enneagram Personality testing is the RHETI or the Riso-Hudson Enneagram Type Indicator. This exam was developed by Don Riso and Russ Hudson in 2000. They devised a systematic method of testing personality types based on the Enneagram model. As such, they were able to develop a scientifically validated test that can accurately determine a person's core personality type.

The RHETI consists of 144 multiple-choice questions. It is generally offered as an online test through the Enneagram Institute (https://www.enneagraminstitute.com/). This organization is focused on providing training and testing services to individuals and companies.

The main difference between the RHETI and the other types of tests mentioned earlier is that the RHETI is a comprehensive evaluation whereas the other free test is an approximation to what your core personality type would. While the free examinations are still rather accurate, they are, by no means, guaranteed to be accurate. Thus, if you are looking for a reliable and scientifically validated means of determining your core personality type, then the RHETI is certainly an option.

According to the Enneagram Institute's website, the cost of taking the RHETI exam is $12 per access code. Each code can be used once. So, if multiple individuals wish to take the test, they would need to pay $12 per person. In exchange for that fee, a rather comprehensive evaluation is performed. Test takes receive quite a bit of information on that personality type and its potential influences. As such, it seems that the information provided is worth the fee that is paid for it.

Ultimately, it is highly recommended that you take at least one of these tests for you to determine your core personality type. The fact of the matter is that whether you choose the free or the paid version of the test, it is important to have an objective means of measuring your personality type. After all, these objective measures can help you establish your starting point.

The one limitation with the free tests is that they don't shed too much light into wings, triads, and levels of personal development in the same way that the full RHETI does. This is why free tests should be taken with a grain of salt. And while the full RHETI is by no means perfect, it is a far more accurate indicator of the full range of variables that play into the Enneagram core personality types.

If you would like to pursue further testing, taking a test such as the Myers-Biggs can also serve as another accurate measure in which you can compare and contrast the results of the RHETI. However, most corporations and private individuals for that matter have found the Enneagram to be a much simple and equally accurate measure.

Also, the RHETI tends to be a more cost-effective option insofar as the fee for the administering of the test is lower and takes a lot less time to perform as compared to a full-blown Myers-Biggs. Notwithstanding, if you, or your organization, have the time and can spare the cost, both tests would certainly be a worthwhile exercise.

One other important point to consider is that neither of these tests will give you an absolute, 100% description of your personality. As mentioned earlier, there is a myriad of factors that have molded and shaped your personality. Hence, it is important to account for these factors were reading through your core personality type.

So, it certainly pays to take a closer look into who you are, and how you got here. One very useful and valuable exercise, especially among family members and groups of co-workers, is to have a meeting to sit down and share results. By sharing results, everyone can get a better understanding of what drives on personality type, what their fears are, as well as, their negative and positive traits. This can lead to a deeper understanding of everyone in that group. At the end of the day, that is the main focus of this exercise: to improve relationships, both at a personal level, and a broader social level.

Chapter 16

The Enneagram and You

In this chapter, we are going to take a deeper look at the real-world applications of the Enneagram and how it can benefit you in the pursuit of your personal goals.

The main purpose of the Enneagram is to foster personal development. As seen in the lines of personal development, the Enneagram is designed to help you determine your starting point and where you can go from there. Even if you start at level 1 or level 9, there is always room for improvement. By the same token, there is always a chance that you could descend even further.

But barring those negative aspects, the Enneagram is meant to help you gain a better understanding of what makes you tick and what drives those around you. This is very important to keep in mind as understanding those around you is the best way to improve overall relationships. It can even help repair damaged or broken relationships since mutual understanding and acceptance are some of the keys to building healthy relationships.

Over time, your understanding of the core personality types will make it easier to deal with new folks. For example, part of the induction process of a new employee could be to take a simple, free Enneagram test. With the result, you can then better help the new co-worker become accustomed to their new surroundings.

When you see the results of this test you can say, "Oh, Mary is a Type Three". Then, you can better help Mary find her place in the company. Perhaps Mary thrives under pressure. Perhaps Mary chooses to avoid conflict. Or, perhaps Mary is a protector. Whatever the case, you can help Mary situate herself in a role, regardless of her actual job functions, that can help her make the best of her attributes.

This is why companies rely heavily on these types of tests. They use them to foster harmonious working relationships among employees and peers. This is a crucial element to consider especially when there are communication problems present in the workplace.

There have been many instances in which a company with communication issues decides to bring in a consultant to perform a test of this nature. Then, upon the results, co-workers are grouped into their core personality types. With this in mind, many folks come to the realization that they avoid responsibility, not because they are lazy or unmotivated, but because they are afraid of failure. So, the focus then shifts on how to better support this colleague as opposed to labeling them as lazy or uncooperative.

By the same token, there might be aggressive individuals in the company who lash out at others, not because they are mean or wish to harm others, but because that is the way they deal with their insecurities and issues. Often, this understanding is enough to diffuse a potential conflict in the workplace. Furthermore, it can help repair damaged relationships especially when significant conflict has taken place.

In other cases, more proactive and open leaders are willing to be transparent so that their subordinates can learn more about their boss' personality. This can help subordinates understand why a leader is permissive, demanding or even jealous. As such, this allows seeing where everyone is standing. In many ways, it's a means of playing on a level field.

On a personal level, the Enneagram is a great tool for self-discovery.

Many folks go through life wondering why they are the way they are, and why they feel the way they do. Often, this leads to large amounts of unnecessary stress. After all, not understanding why things are the way they are can be an enormous source of stress. Many people go through life trying to make sense of the things they do. Often, the answers don't come quite as easily as they would hope. This leads to further frustration and anguish.

As we saw in the levels of personal development, it is easy to fall into a trap of coping mechanisms. Everything from substance abuse, alcoholism, addiction to prescription medication and reliance on food can all lead to harmful coping mechanisms. Naturally, this does far more harm than good.

Nevertheless, when a person can make sense of their fears and their drivers, they can then begin to make far more progress based solely on their understanding of what drives them and what scares them. Indeed, gaining this understanding is a powerful force.

If you are reading this, as we speak, then you have already embarked upon a journey of self-discovery which will be hard to turn back on. By coming this far, you are acknowledging that there is far more to you than what meets the eye. Perhaps you have accepted the fact that there are aspects in your life which you wish to improve, but perhaps don't know where to begin.

Additionally, your road to self-discovery will take different paths. For instance, you may take a plunge before you can reemerge as a new person. Perhaps you might take a few dives before you can find peace and stability. We all go through it. But it is a lot worse when you have no idea why such things occur.

In this journey of self-discovery and self-improvement, it is important to keep your lines of integration and disintegration in clear sight.

We are constantly surrounded by circumstances that can, at one point or another, derail our efforts of making progress within our self-improvement. For instance, the loss of a loved one, an illness, or perhaps major setbacks such as losing a job or falling into financial distress can all derail any progress made toward finding a better emotional state. However, this is where your discovery will help you stay in tune with your feelings.

Let's consider this situation:

You are prone to using alcohol as a coping mechanism. While you are not an alcoholic, you tend to have a little too drunk to drink when you are feeling stressed out. Before gaining this knowledge, there wasn't much you could to do help it. But now that you do have this knowledge, you can identify the onset of such feelings. You are now capable of getting a better handle of the way you feel. Consequently, you can find a better way of handling your feelings as opposed to managing them with alcohol.

If you are the type that internalizes shame, you can better identify those feelings whenever they creep up. For example, if you are prone to blaming yourself for everything that happens, then you can take the time to ask yourself if everything that happens is your fault. You can ask yourself if you did everything you could have done to prevent the things that happened. Perhaps none of it was your fault yet you choose to blame yourself anyway.

By gaining greater insight into these feelings, you can avoid blaming yourself for everything that happens to you. Perhaps you are a victim in reality as opposed to the aggressor. By the same token, you can realize that the things that happen are your fault and you are responsible for them. Of course, this isn't about assigning blame. Quite the opposite, it is about being honest with yourself. At the end of the day, you don't need to show anything to anybody. There is nothing to prove. The only person whom you need, to be honest with is yourself. Others around you will feed off that honesty you have within yourself. Slowly, but surely, things will begin to fall into place.

At this point, you have everything you need to get started in the world of the Enneagram of Personality. You will find that the deeper you dig into it, the more fascinating it becomes. There is no denying that the insights that this model provides are extremely useful. While not 100% accurate, they are accurate enough to set you on a course in which you will find that your understanding of your personality, your motivators, and your fears will indeed set you free. Of course, changes do not occur overnight. However, the biggest step you can take is to open the door to self-discovery.

The ultimate goal of the Enneagram and this book for that matter is to get you on that road to self-discovery. As discussed with the lines of disintegration, one event can set you off the rails. But with the lines of integration, the opposite is true. Perhaps this book will be the catalyst that you have been looking for. Perhaps this message is what you need to get you back on track and the path to integration. Sure, it will not be easy. Yes, there will be some bumps along the way, but is that what makes this whole process fun?

Well, perhaps not fun, but certainly worthwhile. Please spare no efforts in improving yourself. There is always something which you can do to both improve yourself and achieve your goals. You can go about building yourself and your life one day at a time.

Conclusion

Thank you for reading this book. If you made it this far it is because you are truly interested in learning how the Enneagram of Personality can help you improve yourself and your relationships with those around you. Indeed, the Enneagram model can help you gain insights into yourself, and the people in your social group, that you might not have been able to achieve otherwise.

The fact of the matter is that the road to self-discovery is never easy. In fact, you may uncover some issues which may not be the most comfortable or the most pleasant. Yet, they are necessary to reveal. As has been stated before, there is nothing you need to prove to anyone but yourself. You only need to prove to yourself that you are committed to becoming the best possible version of yourself.

That can only happen when you are committed to making the most of the circumstances around you. If you don't feel like you have the knowledge you need, then the Enneagram model is the tool you need in order to get started.

What if you are experienced in your journey of self-discovery?

Then, the Enneagram will surely function as a very useful tool to complement the breakthroughs which you have already made. After all, nothing is perfect in this world. It is quite probable that this tool will help you uncover some deeper aspects of yourself that you might not have been aware of. Perhaps you might simply confirm aspects about yourself that you have been contemplating but perhaps couldn't quite place a finger on.

At this point, the next step to consider is taking the Enneagram personality test. You can begin with any one of the free tests which we have indicated herein. They are a great starting point in which you can determine your core personality. That is the foundation of the Enneagram. Without understanding your core personality, it will be quite hard for you to gain a strong foothold in your understanding of the Enneagram model.

As you progress through the discovery of your core personality, you may very well find aspects about yourself that you might not have previously thought were there. Perhaps you might be filled with Aha! moments.

The fact of the matter is that by starting off with a personality test, you can begin to place your feelings, ideas, reactions, motivators, and fears into a clearer context. These tests can help you to focus your attention on where it would be most useful.

Then, you can move onto more specific aspects such as the influence of your wings. Given the fact that wings are secondary influences into your main character, there is no doubt that studying them in greater detail will also provide you with the elements you need to get a much broader picture of who you are.

Naturally, the Enneagram will never paint a 100% accurate picture of who you are. There will be holes that need to be plugged. Those are more specific aspects which you can look into as you go through your life experience. For example, you fell off your bike as a child and broke your arm. This traumatic experience may explain why you don't like sports despite your personality type being very active. Perhaps your personality type is not prone to discipline, yet you had a very structured upbringing.

All of these aspects which are the product of your environment and your upbringing are all key elements that will help to round out the full picture of who you are. Hence, this is the reason why we say that the journey to self-discovery is not a short one.

If you feel compelled to dig even further into your Enneagram type, you can certainly look into taking the RHETI. The RHETI test is a great way in which you can get a very accurate picture of who you are, your levels of personal development, your wings and even your place in the triad. While the cost of this test is not prohibitive, you may choose to pay the fee or stick with the free versions out there.

Regardless of your choice, taking an Enneagram personality test is the best way in which you can get an objective assessment of your personality type. From there, you can share the information which you have learned with your friends, family, and co-workers. They will surely be interested in learning more about themselves and how to get along with those around them. Sure, there might be some folks who could care less. But the truth of the matter is, most people are always interested in learning more about themselves. Now, not everyone might be ready to face some of the unpleasantness that comes with self-discovery. Nevertheless, this could be the kickstart they need to get on the tracks of their lines of integration.

So, do take the time to share this message with anyone you feel would benefit from it. Perhaps you can all take the Enneagram personality test and embark on this journey of self-discovery as a unit. Often, having a buddy to urge you on is a great way of helping you keep your motivation high. Perhaps you can be the one to help others stay on the road to self-discovery and self-improvement. That is something which you can discover in your own personality type.

As always, please share your comments on this matter. Other readers, out there may be interested in this topic, yet they may not know where to start. As such, your comments will be valuable in helping them see the value in this book.

Hopefully, you have found the information in this book to be useful and insightful. So, please do share your ideas with others around you. They will surely be interested in knowing what you have to say on this topic. After all, there are no better recommendations than those that come from folks who have experience, firsthand, the value in this book.

If you enjoyed this book, please let me know your opinion by leaving a short review on Amazon. Thanks!

The Power

OF

Stoicism

JOHN TURNER

Introduction

Thanks for choosing this book about Stoicism. I'd really love to hear your opinion, so make sure to leave a short review on Amazon if you enjoy it. It means a lot to me!

Stoicism is not a new-age trend. If anything, it is a way of life practiced by the Romans thousands of years ago. It was a guide to life back then. But how about our world, the 21st-century one we are living in right now? Can Stoicism be used today? From the 80s up until today, modern-day philosophers have all been interested in the works of the founding fathers of Stoicism- Seneca, Nero, Epictetus, as well as Marcus Aurelius and the objective, is to draw on their ideas and repackage them as guidance to live life in today's environment.

Philosophers of Stoicism today, such as William Irvine, Ryan Holiday and Massimo Pigliucci all, write about the benefits of following the Stoic way of life with the conviction that Stoicism practiced daily is the key to a happy and good life which focuses on our mental state and the virtues of being rational. It explores the Ideal life, a life that is in sync with nature and practicing a calm indifference towards events that are out of our control.

Stoicism is a line of philosophy that involves personal ethics and is indoctrinated along with the principle of logic and its views on the natural world. The school of stoicism was founded in 300 BC Greece by Zeno of Citium and is heavily influenced by the teachings of Socrates.

During this time in Greece, Stoicism was immensely popular and flourished for several hundreds of years as a way to live by the different people of diverse backgrounds in Greece. Because of its philosophy, stoics were considered to be cold, passive and stone-like figures.

Despite the phrase 'to remain stoic' or to remain indifferent, the Stoics were anything but indifferent to the reality of life. In truth, they were active participants of the world and they used this philosophy to reason and reach out to others in a state of everlasting joy, tranquility, mental fortitude, and character excellence.

In this book, we will explore the reality of Stoicism, its history and most importantly, the principles of Stoicism.

This book will also attempt to help you use Stoicism in everything you do and weave in Stoic exercises and principles into your daily life.

You will also go through the Stoic view of optimism as well as emotions.

You do not have to baptize yourself a Stoic to practice these values and principles. When you continue reading this book, you will come to understand why. The Greek Stoic philosopher Epictetus put it this way: *"There is only one way to happiness and that is to cease worrying about things which are beyond the power of our will."*

Let's journey into a life philosophy that will help you look at the world differently. Stoic or not, this philosophy can be practiced at any point in our lives.

Chapter 1

Stoicism Defined

To give stoicism a definition to better understand it, stoicism can be defined as a way life that teachers a person methods and ways to maintain a rational, calm state of mind no matter what events unfold in front of us.

Stoicism helps us focus on the things that we all can control- our reaction and actions towards a certain scenario or event. Through this mentality, we can then focus on issues that we can control and not be so worried about the things that we cannot. This is probably why the term 'to remain stoic' was created, which is to remain indifferent no matter what is happening around us. Of course, this definition covers just the tip of the iceberg of what Stoicism is about.

History of Stoicism

Founded in 301 BC, Stoicism has come a long way in its train of thought, infusing thoughts and principles that relate to the modern world. First preachers by Zeno of Citium, a Phoenician merchant Stoicism was first known as Zenonism but eventually became to be known as Stoicism, a change in name based on the location that the followers used to originally meet, which was at Stoa Poikile, also referred to as the Painted Porch.

Followers of this school of philosophy often met in public places where anyone could join the conversation, listen to the preaching and debates. At some point, stoicism was also known as a 'philosophy of the street,' and it was usually ordinary folk who were amongst its biggest followers, together with a small number of aristocrats.

From the get-go and for the next five centuries after that, Stoicism has remained among the most popular and influential schools of philosophy. It is also known as a famous civic discipline in the West and was practiced by all walks of life, all different layers of the community, whether rich or poor. Everyone was in the pursuit of the Good Life.

At some point, Stoicism went under the radar and with it, the core knowledge and principles faded and were almost forgotten until the 1970s when Stoicism was revived again. Stoicism came into the spotlight again because of Cognitive Behavioral Therapy (CBT). Authors like Ryan Holiday and William Irvine used Stoicism philosophical inspiration to write about the need for it in our society today.

Leaders of Stoicism

- Marcus Aurelius

Famously referred to as the last good emperor, Marcus Aurelius was also the most powerful man on earth at that time. He reflected every evening on the day's ongoings and wrote down his thoughts and observations in his diary, which would go on to be published as 'Meditations.' It would become one of the most important, profound and significant sources of Stoic Philosophy.

- Epictetus

Born a slave but become a legend, that is the life of Epictetus. Epictetus was also the teacher to other great minds of ancient Rome such as Marcus Aurelius and founded his school. His teachers have been meticulously recorded by his student, Arrian in the book called Discourses and Enchiridion. Enchiridion, meaning 'ready at hand' is often translated as a handbook and meant to be used like a sword ready to be drawn at the slightest sign of danger or threat. The handbook was a way to deal with life's challenges.

- Seneca

Seneca was known as many things from Rome's best playwright to the wisest broker to Nero's tutor and adviser, Seneca's letters survived and served as some of the most sought-after sources of Stoic philosophy. These manuscripts survived despite being forced to commit suicide by Nero. The documents from these leaders of stoicism form the foundations of Stoicism.

Principles of Stoicism

To understand stoicism is to know its principles.

#1 Living in agreement with Nature

Eudaimonia was the central theme for all ancient schools of philosophy and it was the ultimate goal of life. This ultimate goal of life was the supreme happiness attainable by human beings.

The Good Life that the Stoics refer to summed up the idea as 'living in agreement with nature.' This was the goal and the central slogan of Stoicism.

Living in agreement with nature is about behaving rationally as a human being. We must always aim to live our virtues and apply human reasoning to all our actions. Only when we do this, we truly live in agreement with nature, the way humans are meant to behave.

#2 Living by Virtue

Achieving virtue is the highest good that one can attain as a stoic. There are four cardinal virtues in Stoicism:

- Wisdom or prudence
- Justice or fairness
- Courage or fortitude
- Self-discipline or temperance

Here the term virtue lies in excelling at your own character's strength and applying reason that is in a manner that is both praiseworthy as well as healthy.

Acting according to virtue more often than not, brings about benefits. These benefits, however, should be seen as a bonus rather than the primary motive for your actions. This is why reasoning comes into play. You always apply reason to do the right thing and act according to wisdom, courage, justice, and self-discipline.

On another note, the results of your virtuous actions may not always be positive ones. Which is why you shouldn't make it your main motive. By focusing on what you can control (your actions), you are already practicing virtue.

#3 Only Focus on the things Within your Control

A major part of stoicism is the ability to distinguish what elements and issues or scenarios that we can control or within our power and what elements or situations that are beyond our control or out of our power.

Things that are 'up to us' are usually voluntary choices related to our actions as well as our judgments. Everything else beyond that is not under our control.

For example, if you are trying to lose weight; that is what you can control are your diet and fitness. But you do not have control over the genes that you were born into or other factors such as hormonal imbalance, injuries or illnesses.

The idea here is that we are all responsible for our growth and because all that matters in life are up to us. The takeaway here is to focus on our efforts and attention to the elements that we have greater power over- leave the rest of the universe.

#4 Understanding the Difference between Indifferent, Bad and Good

In Stoicism, bad things, good things, and indifferent things have a stark and extremely vivid difference. Stoics refer to good things such as wisdom, justice, courage, and self-discipline, which are all Stoic virtues. The bad things are those opposite of these virtues, which are cowardice, injustice, folly, and indulgence.

When it comes to indifferent things, it is usually life and death, bad reputation and fame, pleasure as well as pain, poverty and wealthy as well as health and sickness. Stoic indifferent things are the kinds of things the modern society would judge as bad or good. However, in Stoicism, these indifferent things do not play a major role in the quest for the Good Life.

Essentially, indifferent things do no matter whether you are rich or poor, sick or healthy. It does not play a huge role in ultimate happiness. We need to be satisfied with whatever nature gives us and be indifferent towards indifferent things.

#5 Taking Action

You are the master of your ship and to attain the Good Life, you cannot just lay back and expect things to happen as is. To live the Stoic way of life or in other words, the eudaimonic life, you would need to always endeavor to do the right thing. Stoics are known to be doers, but it is not enough only to think about your own life. As a Stoic, you need to take action and do things differently. Stoics must earn a good life by taking the necessary and right actions.

Learning how to live your life should also involve applying these ideas.

#6 Asking What Could Go Wrong?

As humans, we are more prone to think about what could go wrong as opposed to what could go right. So this principle of 'What could go wrong' actually sits nicely among modern society. Stoic thinking is to always prepare oneself for future events to stay calm in the face of adversity.

Take for example if you are planning an event and you have done all that the necessary things that you needed to from managing the guest list to finalizing the caterer, the itinerary, decorations are up. Now, you stand back and ask yourself 'What could go wrong?, or 'What could happen that doesn't go as planned?".

Figuring out what would happen outside the plan can help you prepare a backup plan.

7 Accepting the Outcome of Things Beyond Control

In Stoicism, we are all meant to do the right thing and try our best to get there, but at the same time, we are also meant to accept the outcome of things beyond our control. While we need to give it our all, we also must accept that there are outcomes that are beyond our direct control. This is the key to confidence and trusting in your self.

- To do your extremely best
- Understand that results are beyond your control
- To accept whatever that has happened
- To continue to live and act virtuously

#8 Amor Fati – Love Everything that Happens

Another good principle in Stoicism is called the "art of acquiescence" – to accept rather than fight every little thing.

In most events or scenarios that have taken place especially those that have gone south, we can only change our opinions on them and not the event itself, unless we had a time machine and could go back in time. So, we can only accept what has happened and look forward to these two steps:

To accept that we don't control everything that happens. We simply must accept it.

To not only accept, but even love everything that happens. We simply get to enjoy it. It is hard to feel grateful or happy for something that we never wanted to take place, but things happen for a reason and whether it is the desired effect or an unexpected outcome, it happened specifically for you.

You may not understand why it happened, but eventually, you will and you will see how it benefited you.

#9 Turning Problems into Opportunities

Perception is what shapes our outlook on life, how we see the world around us, how we engage with it and how we interpret the things that happen to us. By now, you already know that in Stoicism, events beyond our control are not seen as good or bad but indifferent.

And our perception towards these events boils down to how we choose to look at them and respond to them- it is all that matters. You may choose to look at yourself as a failure when things don't go according to your way and you do not attempt to not take on that challenge again OR you could learn from these failures and choose to take on the challenge again and improve it for round two.

We are not affected by the actual events but by our judgment of these events.

In Stoicism, you need to:

1. to look at the events objectively
2. choose to use them for their best

How you see these events is so much more important because you can find the good in everything. In Stoicism, it is all about looking at things as an opportunity for growth.

#10 Practising Mindfulness

At the end of the day, you need to be mindful of everything that you do. To live according to the Stoic philosophy, you need to be mindful of the actions you because ultimately, all stoic principles are about being more mindful. This also means that you need to be your very own check and balance- monitoring and observing your thoughts and actions towards situations. You must also be more mindful and aware of each step you take in life. When you practice Stoicism, you need to know when to take a step by from your thoughts and also decide on your best action towards certain scenarios.

Chapter 2

The Benefits of Stoicism

The ultimate life goal for Stoics is to live purposefully and carefully. When we are honest with the way we live, it's anything but difficult to perceive how simple (and normal) it is to spend life by accident.

In Stoicism, the principles we learned in the first chapter can be summarized as:

- To be clear about what your intentions are in everything that you do
- To be thoughtful about your choices
- To be simple in your desires and
- To be content with what you can control

What are the benefits of leading a life based on Stoic principles? Essentially, each benefits differently based on what they are going through at the moment in life, but to give you an idea of what you can expect in this modern-day, here are the benefits associated with Stoicism:

#1 You learn to articulate life with a deeper sense of meaning

How much do you align yourself with your purpose each day? Some of us go about life by taking care of other pressing concerns that are not related to us and eventually, these pressing concerns become our lives. In this time, we have forgotten who we are and what our visions are. What kind of life do you want? What kind of parent do you want to be- the ever-present one or the compassionate one? What about the kind of partner you deem yourself to be- the committed? The activist?

What do you want people to remember you as? What kind of legacy do you want to leave behind?

It isn't wrong to be the things described above because all of these things contribute to a positive outcome. A compassionate parent produces a well-adjusted child. A devoted partner enables their partner to achieve success; a goal-oriented entrepreneur enriches a community.

Essentially, some people will be happy with what they have while others are happy with who they are. Stoicism enables us to appreciate these differences. Better guidance is not about asking what we want but more of the kind of person we want to become. This is your mantra each day.

#2 You become more grateful

Stoicism pushes for virtues and when we live by virtues, we tend to look at the circumstances of our actions. While not all our actions are positive ones, the stoicism belief is to be grateful because life is a balance of positives and negatives.

When we focus on the indifferent things, we do not attach ourselves to the positives or the negatives but recognize the balance of living in agreement with nature.

We all have trouble seeing the gratitude in scenarios and events we encounter each day and it is only because we are not seeing much of what we encounter. It is about looking at ourselves and understanding how fortunate we are to be alive and it is also about looking back in our day today and see what we've accomplished, no matter how little the task, like for example- completing this book. Look back and see what events worked in your favor and also what you learned and how you reacted when things didn't work in your favor.

We all receive either something good or something affirming each day- it depends on how we perceive things.

#3 You learn to live with boundaries

When discussing boundaries here, we are not talking about walls or enclosures we lock ourselves in- whether emotionally, physically, mentally or spiritually. It is not about isolating ourselves or living outside the community. It is about acknowledging what resources we have and how to work with it and these resources are limited time and limited energy.

Let's face, we always face limited time and also limited energy; otherwise, we would be running and doing things all day, every day. Living within our boundaries enables us to manage our time and energy efficiency and this means paying attention to the things that matter the most instead of giving into negativity such as anger, resentment, and worry.

Not giving in to these unhelpful emotions enable us to focus on our vision and the people that matter most in our lives.

Consider looking at your relationships that foster well-being and serve to contribute to the vision in your life. Invest your time and energy in these things that sustain your equanimity and let the rest go.

There is absolutely nothing wrong with being selective about where to invest your time and energy. At the end of the day, it makes you a more useful person not only to your goals and vision but to the community you live in and the people you connect to.

#4 Learn to live with not getting what you want (i.e., create a detachment practice)

This principle helps us to let go of attachment in life and again, living in agreement with nature. It is also to be mindful and be able to understand is still great despite not getting what we want on our wish list.

Life presents itself with enough challenges and we do not need to set ourselves up with even more challenges by fueling it with expectations. Here, the principle of perception is practiced. The thing is, there is absolutely nothing in this life of ours is guaranteed, except death. But this is nothing new- we all know this and there's no point getting depressed about it. We need to embrace it and this should be a driving force to focus and invest in relationships that are meaningful and worth your time, one that we enjoy and hold on to these positive relationships till the end or at least as long as we can.

#5 We learn to apply a control grid

If you feel that there are too many things clouding over you and preventing you from thinking straight or dealing with all sorts of issues, then here is a good time to breathe and get out your graph paper.

Think about principle Amor Fati, Love Everything that Happens, and start listing the things you have complete control over and then the things you have some form of control over and finally, the ones that you have no control over. Be as honest as you can. There are times that these things may be about family, work and finances that you may or may not have control over.

What is the benefit of doing this? Well, for one, you will be more efficient in applying your efforts as well as your time and energy into what you can control.

You will also be able to accept the things that you cannot control and love the things that are happening and enjoy it as it happens.

#6 You learn to accept your life as "on loan."

Stoicism applied well into our modern lives enables us to lead a more simplistic and happy life.

It is always good to take a step back once in a while and look at all that you have done in your life and realize that your life… is all on a loan.

Not to get morbid or anything, but essentially, when you realize that all your work, money, kids, partners, friends, parents, land, talents, possessions, as well as joy and grief, is just temporary, you will truly feel more gratitude and you will be able to enjoy you while it lasts.

Life will continue to go on even when you no longest cease to exist. And this is a good thing- you want people you care and love to continue living without grief or pain. You can file it under religion or you can file it under the metaphysical or you can file this under nature or the laws of evolutions or the meaning of life- whatever you want.

Knowing that life is temporary makes it easier to look at things from a different perspective.

Bottom Line

Stoicism wants us to live life more lightly, more purposefully and more deliberately. It is not about just us and it is not meant to detach ourselves from everything else that is happening around us. When we become more aware of the things that we can control and realize the amount of effort we want to put into our relationships, we become more mindful of our time and our energy as well as our thoughts. We are more tuned in to what life brings us and are happier with our lives.

Chapter 3

Understanding the
Stoic Sense of Emotions

When you continue reading this book, you would find that the overriding theme is how Stoics view disasters or problems as possible opportunities. Sometime even when faced with the death of a dear one, a Stoic will always fall back to the reasoning of 'there is good behind this,' or they would have already thought about the worst-case scenario before it happens, in order for them to look at the current situation with a more rational mind.

But, we're humans and we come with a range of emotions. Wouldn't crying over the love of a friend or family help us in the grieving process? Don't Stoics cry?

In this chapter, we will look into the whole sense of emotions from the Stoic perspective. This chapter is extremely important because only then will you truly understand why Stoics think the way they do. Only then will you grasp the idea of emotions from the Stoical perspective.

In stoicism, there are three 'Good Feelings' that are recognized, which are called *hai eupatheiai* in Greek. These three good emotions are:

- Joy vs. Pleasure
- Wish vs. Appetite

- Caution vs. Fear

These good emotions are contrasted with the three Passions or 'Bad Feelings' in the Stoic philosophy, as explained above.

For many people getting immersed in the philosophy of Stoicism, the main issue that is always brought up is that Stoicism does not allow room for emotions or passions to develop. It promotes the idea that suppresses emotions and advocates an unemotional, apathetic and passionless life.

It is not about Rejecting Emotions, rather its rejecting passions.

Stoics' view on emotions is not the same as how the rest of society views it or defines it. In today's world, the word 'emotions' usually refers to a mental feeling that is often contrasted with reason.

When you understand emotion in this sense, then, according to Sellars, "the Stoics do not reject emotions, they reject passions, and that is quite a different thing."

The Stoics also believed that as human beings, we should:

- Cultivate concern and care as well as the empathy towards family and friends
- Acknowledge that external events will affect us in some way
- That we will have natural reactions towards events such as being shocked or scared

For example, if you heard an explosion, you would probably jump behind a wall- this is not passion.

On another note, if you hear that you may be losing your job, then you're bound to be feeling fearful and anxious- this is passion.

At times like these, the Stoic principle is to eliminate negative reactions by thinking about why. So for instance, say if we lose our jobs, it may not be as bad as we think things would get. It may be a little difficult but not entirely bad the way we think of it in our heads. Ultimately, the Stoics believed that our reactions are usually a result of poor perceptions and poor thinking.

The Stoic's List of Good Passions

The Stoics believe that the only good kind of passions is the ones that are virtues which puts the mind in a healthy state. This is considered the only truthful good and the one thing that can guarantee happiness. Good passions often follow mental climates that produce proper and good reasoning.

As John Stellar quotes it:

> *"THE IDEAL STOIC LIFE IS THUS FAR FROM UNEMOTIONAL IN THE ENGLISH SENSE OF THE WORD"*

In this principle, the Stoics reject the faulty reasoning that is a result of judgments that are confused with positive values and all the negative consequences that comes with it.

What is Passion to the Stoic?

To summarize a little bit, so we are all on the same understanding, our modern sense of emotions is not the same as what the Stoics refer to.

The word emotion is Passion in Stoicism, but since we are all more comfortable using the modern word emotion, for this next discussion, we will continue referring to **Passion = Emotion**.

To make it easier, we will go with **EorP**.

The first definition relates to EorP being an impulse or force. These things happen to anyone and are often contrasted with the things we do or the actions we take.

For example, EorP is like running downhill but not being able to stop. Instead, the force propels you forward. EorP also has a temporal dimension which is usually strong at present and over time, it starts to weaken. On the 2nd or 3rd definitions, it emphasizes greatly on disrupt reasons.

Often, EoPr misrepresents an item's value and this then misleads our impulses towards wanting to achieve it. For instance, let's look at wealth. Pursuing it without being mindful only leads to a life lived poorly as we lack all the goodness that comes with life.

On another instance, say if we want to take revenge on someone and we act on it based on an angry impulse, this means that it could lead us to commit a crime (since we did not think about this rationally in the first place) and the consequence would be dealing with the law and ending up in jail.

EorP is based on bad reasoning.

The last definition of EorP is as "a fluttering in the soul." This definition is derived from Stoic's sense that EorP has a physical basis, which leads to a physical consequence. It is like a relationship between heart rate and blood pressure

In most Stoic teachings, you will often find that the primary Passions that the Stoics identify with are related to appetite and fear. The general idea is if we think of something is good and pure, we tend to pursue it, but when we think of something is not good or bad, we end up fearing it.

These Passions, according to the Stoics, are often related to either Distress or Pleasure. When we satisfy our appetites, we experience pleasure, but when we fail to satisfy them, we end up getting distressed over it. If we end up fearing something, we also end up feeling distressed, but when this fear does not manifest or happen the way we imagine it to be, then we experience pleasure.

Is having too much of emotions bad for us?

Any kind of excessive emotion, if you think about it- is bad. Anything excessive is bad and you probably didn't need the Stoics to tell you that. Experiencing EorP excessively can cause errors in judgment whether it is between the bad and the good, the past, the present or the future.

At first, it may seem pleasurable, but eventually, it will become bad for us. Excessive EorP brings about bad judgments. If our satisfaction for appetites for things like food and drink, material possessions or even sex brings us less pleasure than we anticipated, this could mean that you have indulged in it too much.

The Stoics believed that it isn't worth the risk for more important things such as health in the pursuit of bad passions. In another way, the things that we fear, such as pain, anxiety, and humiliation may not be as bad as we thought. We cannot stop living just because we are paralyzed with fear.

The Role of Emotions

The Stoics never rejected Passions but strive towards living a balanced emotional life. If you think of pleasure, the Stoics think of it as joy. If you think of it as fear, the Stoics think of it as caution. If you feel there's appetite, the Stoics look at it as reasonable hope. As for distress, the Stoics reject it completely.

You should act as a result of rational deliberation. For example, you may want to lead a healthier lifestyle but do not attempt to run every day or take heavyweights- this is considered excessive. If you are considering living by the principles of Stoicism, then it is maybe hard at first to draw the line between excessive and restrained EorP. But, as you practice a balance, you will live a better life when reason prevents us from becoming slaves to our passions and desires.

Calmness in the Face of Adversity

Sometimes, whether we like it or not, we get sucked into other people's drama or get involved in office politics or we are affected by the issues that are happening in our community.

Most of the time, we did not ask to be involved or to be sucked in or to be affected. Things just happen. Negativity spreads like cancer and as much as you do not like it, you end up having to deal with it or having to deal with the consequences of it.

Imagine a life where the things that trouble everyone else did not trouble you?

What if you lived a life when everyone else got mad or upset or greedy but you like a champion, remained calm, clear-headed and objective?

Well, in truth, you can be this way. That is what Stoicism strives to educate its followers on. The Stoic ideas seek to give you plenty of power, the coolness of a cucumber and the serenity of a calm mind.

Your top priority goal is to build an inner fortress that enables you to stay calm and even untouchable when you are faced with adversity. You do not need to give into events excessive attention than what it already has. We do not want to be slaves to our impulses and be pushed around by external events.

This is not easy to do but with some practice, effort, and know-how, we can get closer to this unflappable calmness.

#1 Concern yourself with only your actions

"HAPPINESS AND FREEDOM BEGIN WITH A CLEAR UNDERSTANDING OF ONE PRINCIPLE: SOME THINGS ARE WITHIN OUR CONTROL, AND SOME THINGS ARE NOT. IT IS ONLY AFTER YOU HAVE FACED UP TO THIS FUNDAMENTAL RULE AND LEARNED TO DISTINGUISH BETWEEN WHAT YOU CAN AND CAN'T CONTROL THAT INNER TRANQUILITY AND OUTER EFFECTIVENESS BECOME POSSIBLE."
– EPICTETUS

All of us can be so many good things from good to kind, patient to forgiving. But no matter what we do, we cannot control the outcome of these actions. Life has a wicked sense of humor. You may think you're doing all the right things, but then your partner will leave you. You may think you're being the best team player in your department only to be let go by management. You may think that you're eating the best and healthier food, but you'd end up with cancer. Rather than worrying yourself about that what-ifs and what mays which you cannot control, you can just look inside you and control only your character, your actions, and your reactions.

How you act and treat people may not necessarily influence the way they will treat you. You may be kind and helpful, but this does not mean all of them will appreciate your kindness and goodness. Your patience will be tested and even your love towards your partner questioned. These are outcomes you have no control of and in no way would be able to influence. You also have no control over what people think of you. Some may react in the way you envision, but some may think otherwise of you. You can influence them, but you cannot control their actions or thoughts or opinions about you. The only thoughts and opinions you can control are that of your own.

#2 Do good without thinking if it will be noticed

*"An emerald shines even if its worth is not spoken of." — **Marcus Aurelius***

If you want to do well, do well but don't look and see if others can see the goodness you are doing. Do good because they are good and not because you want to be liked or loved or even respected.

When it comes to doing good in the Stoic book, you'd be surprised that it mirrors the kind of teachings we've all heard of before. When it comes to doing good work, for the Stoic, it's all about doing good hard work because hard work is good and not because it will bring you good things.

When it comes to love, love because giving your love to someone is a good thing, not because you also want to be loved back.

When it comes to being fair to others, do it because it is the right thing to do and not because you expect to be treated the same way should the time come.

You want to do something because the reward is just that it is good and not because you want something out of it. Only you can control your goodness so your efforts and energy should be focused on you.

#3 Do not blindly accept or reject criticism

> *"If someone can show me that what I think or do is not right, I will happily change, for I seek the truth, by which no one was ever truly harmed. It is the person who continues in his self-deception and ignorance who is harmed."*
> *— Marcus Aurelius*

Evaluate the criticism you receive and change for the better. You were not made perfect and acknowledging this is the first step to self-improvement. We can lead a calmer more serene life if we know that deep down, we have made the best effort to become a better version of ourselves.

As long as we are putting in an honest effort to improve, our conscience will be clear. Do not dig a hole of self-deception because this is ultimately a trap that we create for ourselves. It tears down and claws us down when we least expect it. This leads us into a dark abyss of certainty, where we do not know what troubles us.

#4 Do not fear the unknown

"WILD ANIMALS RUN FROM THE DANGERS THEY SEE, AND ONCE THEY HAVE ESCAPED THEM WORRY NO MORE. WE, HOWEVER, ARE TORMENTED ALIKE BY WHAT IS PAST AND WHAT IS TO COME. A NUMBER OF OUR BLESSINGS DO US HARM, FOR MEMORY BRINGS BACK THE AGONY OF FEAR WHILE FORESIGHT BRINGS IT ON PREMATURELY. NO ONE CONFINES HIS UNHAPPINESS TO THE PRESENT."
– SENECA

The Stoics believe that people are born with only two fears, which are the fear of falling and the fear of loud noises. The rest of our fears originate from our past and these fears become a reality in our future. We are rarely ever afraid of the things in our present. We may fear loneliness not because we are alone today, but we fear that we may be forever alone.

#5- Train to focus your thoughts and goals

"TO BE EVERYWHERE IS TO BE NOWHERE." –
SENECA

Low attention spans, wanderlust, fear of commitment are all the human desire to be everywhere or risk the fear of missing out.

With the internet, we are more unfocused than we were before because it enables us to be everywhere at once and yet at the same time, nowhere. The more and more we are hounded by mobile phones and laptops, smartphones and other gadgets, we lose our ability and desire to focus.

It isn't to say that you MUST always focus on one thing or only be one certain place all the time or hang out with just one person. The mind also needs relaxation to explore your thoughts.

Thinking about too many things and too many issues can be detrimental. Having an aimless mind with your location always changing and your options always open, you will run into purposelessness. You will end up being everywhere but nowhere and this does not make for an interesting person nor a calm person. You will find out that not one thing or one place can ever satisfy you.

#6 Control your mind and your attitude

"IF YOU WANT TO ESCAPE THE THINGS THAT
HARASS YOU, WHAT YOU'RE NEEDING IS NOT TO

People are often led to believe that the reason for their unhappiness is because of the circumstance that they are in. They are always led to believe that if only they had one chance in a pleasant situation, they would be much happier.

However, as mentioned before, you will never be able to control a situation you are in full.

Life at any given moment can take a turn for the worst and while this is something that you cannot control, you can, however, control your mind and attitude towards this scenario. Never let anything or anyone harass you without your permission- you can deny this at any given moment.

Practice Misfortune (Ask What Could Go Wrong)

As humans, we are more prone to think about what could go wrong as opposed to what could go right. So this principle of 'What could go wrong' actually sits nicely among modern society.

Stoic thinking is to always prepare oneself for future events to stay calm in the face of adversity.

According to William Irvine, author of the book A Guide to the Good Life, described it as "the single most valuable technique in the Stoics' toolkit" and termed it 'negative visualization.' the only difference is that these scenarios of what could go wrong are not negative ones, but they are 'indifferent'.

Take for example if you are planning an event and you have done all that the necessary things that you needed to from managing the guest list to finalizing the caterer, the itinerary, decorations are up. Now, you stand back and ask yourself 'What could go wrong?', or 'What could happen that doesn't go as planned?'.

Figuring out what would happen outside the plan can help you prepare a backup plan.

Negative Visualization as a Powerful Tool

Negative visualization deals with one of the most important issues in Stoicism, which is to prepare for anything and everything that may come your way.

It is sort of like foresight. Before something could happen, Stoics look at the possibilities of what could go wrong or what obstacle may crop up or what difficulties could happen.

In using negative visualization, there are three elements we can look at, which are:

1. What's the key idea?
2. Why it wasn't actually 'negative' to the Stoics.
3. Why so pessimistic?

What's the Key Idea of the Stoic Exercise 'Negative Visualization'?

The idea is clear and simple. All you need to do is to visualize the possibility of something going wrong. You are putting out all the scenarios that could go wrong so that if they occur, you will stay calm and cool. Staying calm and cool enables you to respond in the best way possible.

A stoic's main goal is to attain the Good Life and to reach is that to live following virtues from courage to wisdom, justice, and temperance. To live according to these virtues, Stoics mentally train themselves.

In all honesty, it is easy to live according to virtues when life goes on as planned. But would you still be able to when things don't go on as planned, such as when you encounter illness or death or exile?

By regularly visualizing misfortunes, Stoics prepares for the worst and lives in a virtuous manner when they have occurred and they referred to this exercise as premeditation Malorum to train themselves to stay calm and free despite the emotional suffering that they face or when bad situations have happened.

Modern Stoic philosopher, William Irvine was the one who coined the term 'negative visualization,' and by practicing to visualize negative scenarios, we decrease our fear for them and prepare ourselves to deal with the crises that occur. This kind of exercise is also used in Cognitive Behavioral Therapy (CBT).

Are the Misfortunes Imagined in Negative Visualization Really "Negative"?

Again, it is understandable if someone misconstrues the term negative visualization to mean something bad. It is misleading, no doubt.

But the thing is, the basic Stoic principle points out that external events can neither be positive nor negative but only indifferent, simply because they are out of our control.

The Stoics prefer focusing on what is within their control and not worrying about the things that are beyond their control. This is why the Stoics imagined as well as real 'misfortunes' are just not only negative ones but the ones that they do not have control over.

To put it in simple terms, the bad things that we imagine aren't bad, but it has got to do with our response and reaction to it.

How to Practice Negative Visualization Step by Step

Before we move ahead on how to practice negative visualization, a quick reminder that negative visualization isn't just about preparing yourself to face the worst possible scenarios but also facing events and situations that you have no control of.

For example, a bad or negative situation could be the loss of a spouse. You get married and you are well aware that one day, either one of you will die. As a Stoic, you visualize what could happen in the event of spousal death. Before anything could occur, you prepare for the worst but ensuring that you both have your wills written, determine who gets what, how your properties would be divided, what happens to your retirement fund and bank accounts, what happens to your children and possessions.

A situation that you have no control of would be something like the electricity going off on one of your events. You plan everything from the decor to the napkins, making sure the chef cooks the steak as requested by all your guests, you make sure every bulb in every chandelier is working, you get the grass cut, the marble floors gleamed and then the day of the event happens and then, it suddenly goes dark. What do you do?

As a Stoic, you keep calm and rationalize the situation at hand. You have your electrician on standby- get them to check the circuits. Have you a generator on standby to- turn it on to bring lights to the main areas of the event while the electrician works on the circuits. You also prepared candles- get them out and charm your guests to dine under the soft lights of candles for a romantic night.

This is what negative visualization prepares us for. We ask what could go wrong in advance so that before a launch of a product, a start of a road trip or a commute to a job interview- you have plan B in case something should happen.

So to practice negative visualization, let's pull out the scenario going on a road trip.

Instead of imaging a most likely to happen scenario, try instead to imagine the worst-case scenario and the things that could go wrong, even if it is unlikely it could happen (like the Avenger's Civil War happening in your neighborhood).

Think of these scenarios as if it is happening at the very moment and not in the future. (The Avengers are fighting right about now)

What do you do in a situation like this? You're already in your van and someplace in the middle of town trying to get out to the freeway. What is the best you can do? Well, you can focus on what YOU CAN DO instead of panicking. Maybe wait till traffic subsides? Or find an alternative route out.

You can use the steps above to help you visualize what to do in an upcoming situation that you are getting yourself into. You will feel better prepared, mentally and physically.

We can work up an active and wild imagination, so visualizing these scenarios would be fairly easy.

You can also practice negative visualization as a post-mortem to an event. For example, the case of your spouse dying and you are overwhelmed with grief and sadness. What do you do? You prepare for dealing with these emotions by telling yourself that it was good while it lasted, that you enjoyed the times you had with them. It may not help immediately, but it will help in getting you out of a depressed mental state.

Conclusion

Negative visualization can be used at any time and for any specific events that you feel may incur some problems happening if you do not prepare for it beforehand. We can also do it periodically with general situations and events.

Chapter 4

Reemergence of Stoicism in the 21st Century

Stoic teachings during the Middle Ages were generally related to issues concerning social and political focus. It eventually evolved in the Renaissance era with much of its focus geared towards Roman and Greek relics, to give a substratum to the second happening to Stoic perspectives in rationale, epistemology, and mysticism. This is the same for the documentation of the more recognizable Stoic conventions in morals and legislative issues. When it comes to the development of Stoicism towards the 21st century, here are some notable philosophers you need to know about:

- Justus Lipsius

Philosopher, humanist and philologist, Lipsius was a 16th century Flemish that was one of the revivers of Stoic doctrines. His most famous work is *De Constantia*. His teachings also influenced a great many people, one of whom was the Baron de Montesquieu and political theorist Charles-Louis.

- Guillaume du Vair

A 17th-century French Christian lawyer and philosopher who focused his research and understanding of the Stoic moral code of conduct and made this version popular at the time. Together with him was Pierre Charron, the French skeptic, and theologian.

- Francis Bacon

Popularly recognized as the advocate of Lipsius teachings, he also encouraged the Stoic teachings related to modern philosophies of science. In the later Middle Ages, Stoicism doctrines also influenced many prominent figures in the Reformation and Renaissance periods, especially in the continuing war against Aristotelianism.

- Pietro Pomponazzi

This 16th-century philosopher defended anti-scholastic Aristotelianism against the rising Averroists. Pomponazzi had strong Aristotelian roots and through his understanding of Stoicism, he adopted and advocated the Stoic view of freedom of will and providence.

- Leonardo Bruni

Like Pomponazzi, Bruni also adopted and advocated Stoic views regarding reason, fate, and fate-will. Bruni is a 15th-century humanist.

During this period, between the 15th and 16th centuries, there were plenty of books written about the philosophy of public law with a special focus on human nature and Stoic principles.

These books, such as De Jure Belli's 'On the Law of War & Peace' as well as Utopia by Thomas More and Hugo Grotius all discuss social rights, the theory of natural law and the Good Life of Stoicism.

- Huldrych Zwingli

Sixteenth-century Swiss reformer was a great advocate of subjective conviction as the new element of Christianity, which was in line with Stoic perspectives. This was especially related to the unrestrained choice and also on the outright destiny of the great and terrible individual, and moral determinism.

- Herbert of Cherbury

Also known as the father of Deism would go on to develop the ideation of religious peace and the reducing of opposing views on religion, which are common elements. This view was soon to gain popularity and become a main theme in the 17th century.

- Philipp Melanchthon

This philosopher was also a great advocate of humanism and antiquity. The main motivation for him was Aristotle even though Melanchthon likewise took a gander at the Stoic hypothesis of information which trusts those inborn standards and the regular light of reason, which instructs the considerable certainties of mystical and good request.

Eventually, Stoicism was made the basis of the natural-law theory which reasons that the state is of direct divine origin and the independence of the church

In the seventeenth century, the Cartesian unrest acquired other Stoic understandings, for example, that profound quality is a mix of dutifulness to the law of reason, which God has presented to people morals surmises an intelligence of nature since people must figure out how to keep their place on the planet, for at exactly that point may they act appropriately

This self-checking is the premise of morals and the shared trait of truth bespeaks the view that lone considerations and will have a place with people as the body is of the material world. These perspectives were created by René Descartes and he is regularly hailed as the father of present-day reasoning, in his dualism of brain (or soul) and body.

- Benedict de Spinoza

Jewish patriot and ardent advocate of freedom of will made homogeneous usage of Stoic perspectives on the idea of people and the world.

- Blaise Pascal

French religious logician and researcher were, at this time, attempting to align the Cartesian ideas of human origins of instinct. His religious idea held both the Stoic and Cathesian emphasis on the autonomy of rationalizing and reasoning, holding that people are on a very basic level reasoning creatures, intrinsically fit for settling on the right choices.

Stoicism has, in general, contend a huge part throughout the ages within the system development of Christian thought further as in Christian ideas, up to date philosophy has taken from Stoicism, a minimum of partially, its conviction that people, in general, should be created as being proximately and primarily connected with the globe.

Contemporary humanism maintains common Stoic principles like the idea in the commonness of people on the premise of common nature and primary reason. It is maybe simply because Stoicism has never become a comprehensive philosophy that, once several centuries of the dissolution of the Stoic College, foundation themes of its philosophy have neem re-emerging and plenty of it became incorporated into trendy philosophy.

Chapter 5

Masters of Stoicism Then and Now

In this chapter, we will take an in-depth look at the various masters of Stoicism with a description of who they are, notable works as well as lessons from each of them. Understanding who these ancient masters are enables anyone to have a deeper connection to Stoicism and the processes that it went through to where Stoicism is in our modern world today.

Seneca

Seneca's philosophy narrowed on the issue of riches and wealth. It seems to be contradicting for a Stoic philosopher to become, at one point, among the richest in Rome. This juxaposition itself sets him as a unique figure and worth to study. Over 2,000 years ago, Seneca was born in a quiet town in Southern Spain and then moved to Rome to be educated.

In his youth, Seneca focused on politics and have become an upper-level finance clerk. Additionally, he wrote a number of his well-known works like the Consolation to Marcia.

Around 41 A.D with Claudius becoming the emperor, Seneca's life took a drastic turn and he was exiled by the emperor due to allegations of adultery with the emperor's niece.

While his time in exile, Seneca wrote a letter to console his mother while he was in exile. It would be 8 years before Seneca returns to Rome thanks in part to Agrippina, wife of Claudius and mother to future emperor Nero who has asked for Seneca to become Nero's tutor and advisor.

Nero would grow up to become one of the most tyrannical and notorious emperors in the Roman Empire history, which then raised more concerns about Seneca's character. Seneca's wealth was largely in part through his service as Nero's educator. Seneca's death is also in part to Nero's orders who were under the impression that Seneca was part of a plot to assassinate Nero, replacing him with Gaius Piso. Seneca died in 65 AD. Stoicism remained constant in Seneca's life, despite all the turbulent episodes in his personal life.

Seneca's introduction to Stoicism is from Attalus, who was also a Stoic philosopher and among Seneca's early teachers. Seneca was also a Cato admirer, but he did not only confine himself to Stoicism. Seneca, in his writings and teachings, borrowed liberally from other schools of thought such as from Epicurus.

Seneca's influence grew after his death with notable figures quoting and learning from his such as Francis Bacon, Erasmus, Montaigne, and Pascal. Strong interest in him also continued in modern-day Stoicism and one of the biggest quotes is from author and trader, Nassim Taleb, who dedicates a whole chapter to Seneca in his book. Tim Ferriss, entrepreneur and writer who published an audiobook also sites Seneca.

He understood well enough that he was not perfect and went through difficult paths in life. Seneca's life is one colored with the ideals of politics to power, ambition to wealth. Despite it all, he is also extremely well known for his introspective understanding and self-awareness of life and subjects of philosophy.

Works & Readings by Seneca

Seneca's writings and work have been declared as among the most enjoyable and readable works compared to other ancient philosophers. This is in part due to most of his work being in the form of letters. If you want to explore more of Seneca's work, here are some recommendations for you:

On the Shortness of Life

This is a trilogy of short letters that offer one of the best introductions of who Seneca is as a philosopher. On the Shortness of Life, he talks about TIME as a non-renewable element in our lives. His most famous quotes from this letter are "We are not given a short life, but we make it short, and we are not Ill-supplied but wasteful of it."

Letters from a Stoic

Seneca was one who gave excellent advice to those who seek it from him. These letters make for profound reading and you can also use them as a guide to help you overcome the problems you face in life from grief, despair, depression, success and other issues we deal with. You can read or listen to these writings through audiobooks which you can listen to the collection "The Tao of Seneca" produced by Tim Ferriss.

You can also look at Seneca's plays, Dying Every Day, which offers an excellent biography of Seneca. Look out for Antifragile that contains a dedicated chapter of him by Ferriss. If you are looking for something more scholarly, then the academic paper "Seneca on Trial" offers more in-depth readings.

Lessons and Exercises from Seneca

#1 Find a Role Model

In this correspondence to Lucilius, Seneca urges him to choose the right role model who can provide a good standard of living. This idea is not unique to Stoicism - Stoics do have a role model to emulate. However, Seneca stresses the reason and importance of it. The person we choose to emulate can provide us with the right principles that enable us to navigate through the most difficult and trying of times. It also sets standards for ourselves so we can be the judge of our behavior.

#2 Never Be a Slave of Your Worldly possessions

Although Seneca was known for his wealth as well, he was known to be never dependent on it. According to Nassim Taleb, Seneca was the master of his riches and not its slave. Following this observation, we too need to re-examine our relationship with the material possessions that surround us. Are we trapped by it, being so scared to lose it or can we live freely without it? Seneca concluded his attitude of not being a slave but a master of good fortune "For the wise man regards wealth as a slave, the fool as a master."

#3 Fight Your Ego

Seneca was well aware of how the ego can impede our thoughts from progressing and learning. This rings true especially in our day and age where everyone is used to only hearing praise and never criticism. The more praise we get, the more we buy into it, which is how tyrannical leaders are borne. When you keep hearing that you are like God and treated like that, you start to believe it.

Marcus Aurelius

Born nearly two millennia ago, the Roman Emperor Marcus Aurelius was a great leader and a role model, especially on Stoic principles. Born into a prominent family, there was little known of his childhood despite his family being established in Roman society. However, there are greater reports of him as a young man who was into hunting, boxing and wrestling. Hadrian, the reigning emperor at the time of his teenagerhood, was not only old but also heirless, which is why a successor, at the very least, was imperative. Hadrian's first choice, Lucius Ceionius died unexpectedly and so his next choice was Antoninus, a senator at the time who was also childless. As per Hadrian's condition, Antoninus adopted Marcus as well as Ceionius's son, Lucius Verus as his sons and that was how Marcus was known as Marcus Aurelius Antoninus.

Upon Hadrian's death, Marcus was the clear choice as a successor as emperor. His education was the focus and he had the privilege to study under Herodes Atticus, who was a rhetorician from Athens as well as Marcus Cornelius Fronto who taught in Latin. The correspondences between Marcus Aurelius and Marcus Cornelius survives to this day.

Marcus would also serve as a consul twice, which meant he would be receiving a valuable and practical education. When Antoninus died in 161, this ended one of the longest reigns in the Roman

Empire. Marcus Aurelius subsequently became the next Emperor and ruled for another two decades until he died in 180. Marcus's reign was not an easy one. He had to deal with the wars from the Parthian Empire, the barbarian tribes from the North, the rise of Christianity and plagues that killed his people.

Before his death, Marcus made his son Commodus his co-emperor. Cassius Dio, the historian at the time describes Marcus's attitude towards Commodus as "amid unusual and extraordinary difficulties he both survived himself and preserved the empire. Just one thing prevented him from being completely happy, namely, that after rearing and educating his son in the best possible way he was vastly disappointed in him."

Marcus held one of the most powerful positions in the ancient world. He knew that nothing would be off-limits to him so he could if he wanted to, indulge and succumb to temptations. We have known throughout history that absolute power leads to corruption and yet, Marcus did not fall into these temptations and instead, proved himself worthy of the powerful position that he is in.

Historian Edward Gibbon noted in the book 'Five Good Emperors' that under Marcus's reign, the Roman Empire was governed with both virtues as well as true wisdom. It was this that his subjects saw that put in a class above the rest and a huge distinction from the rest of Rome's past leaders and even those that came after him.

Meditations, among his most famous works, was written in the last few years of his life. It contained his most private and intimate thinking of the world and events around him, especially at a time when he was once the most powerful person on earth. He admonished himself on how to be even more virtuous, just, wise and immune to temptation.

Stoicism provided a solid framework for Marcus in dealing with the pressures and temptations of daily life. Marcus embraced the Stoic studies and thanks to his teacher, Rusticus for introducing him to its teachings as well as the Stoic leader Epictetus. Heraclitus was another strong influence on Marcus as well as to Stoicism. The tragic thing about Marcus was, upon his death, the principles which he led Rome by - duty, self-restraint, respect for others- were abandoned by the imperial line.

Works & Readings by Marcus Aurelius

Marcus was known for two things. One, as the last Good Emperor and two, for personal diary Meditations which was never intended for publication. Meditations are touted as one of the greatest books written in history, but it is also the only book of its kind. The writings explore personal ethics, self-discipline, humility, strength, and self-realization on a definitive engagement. It became the source of inspiration for other writers such as Ambrose Bierce and Robert Louis Stevenson as well as for politicians such as Wen Jiabao, Theodore Roosevelt, and Bill Clinton.

Gregory Hays says that for centuries, traces of Mediations were lost until, in the 10th century, it started appearing in scholarly letters. To explore more, you can also read Hays's translation and for further reading- The Inner Citadel and Philosophy as a Way of Life penned by Pierre Hadot which focuses on the studies of men behind the work.

You can also get an in-depth insight into works inspired by Marcus, such as The Obstacle is the Way.

Lessons and Exercises from Marcus

#1 Practice to Exercise your Virtues

When we start telling ourselves that we do not possess certain talents, we begin to start self-pity and, in this process, we miss out on the stuff that we possess. We need to stop ourselves from doing this and instead, focus our energy on things that we already possess inside us, which is our capacity and potential for virtuous action.

#2 Reap Strength from those around you

In Meditations, Marcus wrote notes to himself that served as reminders and in times of challenges and difficulty, he would often write words of encouragement, notes to motivate himself and writings of his duty. If we were to learn from Marcus, that would be the element to draw strength from the people in our lives or look at the people that inspire us.

#3 Focus on The Present

Marcus was aware of all the temptations that existed that would make our imaginations run wild, and envision all the ways that these things could go wrong. This exercise is, of course, useful so we can prepare ourselves for the future and make us ready for any kind of adversity. However, Marcus also knew that crippling fear would prevent us from looking forward and thus, paralyze us from getting into action. While it is always ideal to look at the various touchpoints to prevent disasters from happening, we must also be open to act in the future.

Epictetus

Born 2,000 years ago in Hierapolis as a slave to a wealthy household, Epictetus was permitted by his then owner Epaphroditus to pursue liberal studies. His pursue of liberal studies was what opened Epictetus to the philosophy of Stoicism and further exposure was through the teachings of someone who would eventually become his teacher and mentor, Musonius Rufus.

Soon after, Epictetus obtained his freedom after when Emperor Nero passed away and he began his philosophical teachings in Rome for 25 years. Unfortunately, Emperor Domitian placed a ban on all philosophers from Rome. Epictetus then fled to nearby Greece, settling in Nicopolis, where he began a school and continued teaching till his death.

It is learned that someone purchased Epictetus' earthenware lamp for 3,000 drachmas. The importance of this lamp can be traced to Epictetus's Stoic principle which states: "I keep an iron lamp by the side of my household gods, and, on hearing a noise at the window, I ran down. I found that the lamp had been stolen. I reflected that the man who stole it was moved by no unreasonable motive. What then? Tomorrow, I say, you will find one of earthenware. Indeed, a man loses only that which he already has."

James Stockdale, a POW for 7 years in Vietnam, credits Epictetus for providing him the blueprint of how to endure tortures he was being subjected to. Stockdale recalled Epictetus' disabled leg, which he equated his bound leg as a POW. Stockdale reminded himself of the principle by Epictetus' that physical disabilities are merely an obstacle of the body. It does not need to interfere in our ability to choose unless we make it our choice to choose.

Say this to yourself concerning everything that happens and you will begin to see that these obstacles are mere hindrances to greater things. In author Tom Wolfe's novel, A Man in Full, Epictetus is featured prominently in it and even psychologist Albert Ellis's Cognitive Behavioral Therapy was also influenced by Epictetus teachings.

Epictetus never wrote down his teachings, but it was his student Arrian that has taken up upon himself to have a written account of all these teachings. We can find guidance and strength as well as solace in Epictetus' lessons, it is there if we only choose to read and follow it.

Works & Readings by Epictetus

If you are starting with Epictetus, then his Enchiridion, or 'a small handbook' in English is a good place to begin as it is an excellent introduction to Epictetus as it is full of short Stoic maxims and principles.

Epictetus' book though, is difficult to read unlike the works of Seneca and Marcus. The next book or work to consider would be Discourses, which is a longer read and takes a while to comprehend and understand. You can also start on James Stockdale's autobiography Courage Under Fire if you find Epictetus' works too much of a commitment as a start. There is also A Man in Full by Tom Wolfe.

Lessons and Exercises from Marcus

#1 Keep in mind what you can control

The most important principle is to always remember that there are only certain things that you can control while there is a lot that you cannot. You are reminded not to get upset and angry, especially when it concerns someone else's feelings and events that are outside our ability to control. We need to remind ourselves that only our feelings and our behavior are what we need to check and balance. We are always reminded that we need to let certain things go and accept things as they are, which is key to a more fulfilling life. Yet at the same time, a powerful reminder that our actions and choices are fully in our control.

#2 Set the Standard

Good leaders rarely talk about how things should be done. Instead, they allow their actions to speak for themselves. You need to think about a role model of yours and the lessons that you indirectly received from the choices that they made as well as the examples that they have set in place. In the same essence, we also need to be focused on how we are living and the various choices we make because this will ensure that our energy and time is spent well.

#3 Create a Character for Yourself

Human beings are habitual creatures, which is something Epictetus was very well aware of. We often think that there's only one way to do certain things only because it has become a habit for us. In this sense, Epictetus encourages his students to set principles as well as priorities for themselves to follow. Setting this also prevents people from straying too far from it.

Epictetus was aware of how much we human beings act out of habit and how we think that our ways of doing certain things are set in stone. He encouraged his students to set standards and principles that they are required to follow and not stray far away from it. With daily reminders on which way to take and what choices we ought to make, we eventually become closer to the characters we wish to be and have.

Throughout this book, you have heard plenty of times the names of Epictetus, Marcus Aurelius, as well as Seneca. What about modern-day Stoic gurus? Do they exist? Are their teachings in line with Stoicism? Can I use these values in this modern-day setting?

Modern Day Stoic Thinkers

In this chapter, we will look at some of the brightest stars of Stoicism so you can be able to answer if their values, understanding, and principles can be used in today's world.

If you are new to Stoicism and you are looking for a Guru or a role model to follow and emulate, these modern Stoics can help you understand Stoicism in its modern context. However, understanding the root and foundations of Stoicism is as important as practicing it.

Massimo Pigliucci

Born on 16 January 1964, Pigliucci was a former co-host of the Rationally Speaking Podcast and also the former editor in chief of Scientia Salon, an online magazine. He is an advocate of science education, secularism and a great critique of creationism as well as pseudoscience. He is also a strong advocate for modern Stoicism.

Born in Monrovia, Liberia and raised in Rome, Italy, Pigliucci is a fellow Advancement of Science America and the Committee for

Skeptical Inquiry. He also earned a philosophy of science from the University of Tennessee.

During his tenure as the professor of ecology and evolution at the Stony Brook University, Pigliucci researched genotype-environment interactions, phenotypic plasticity as well as natural selection, focusing on the obstacles in natural selection through genetic and development makeup of organisms.

Pigliucci received the Theodosius Dobzhansky Prize in 1997 while working at the University of Tennessee.

Pigliucci, as a philosopher, is focused and continuously interested in the foundations of evolutionary theory, particularly the relationship between philosophy and science as well as the relationships between sciences with religion. Pigliucci pens his thoughts and opinions regularly for the Skeptical Inquirer and Philosophy Now on topics such as intelligent design, climate change denial, and pseudoscience as well as philosophy.

Massimo's Views on Stoicism

Massimo has been practicing Stoicism for about two years and regularly blogs about his opinions, points of view and information on Stoicism at How to Be A Stoic. His piece in the New York Times of the same name became one of the most shared and viewed articles on Stoicism.

Massimo tried studying Buddhism for a while, but he felt that some parts of it were too alien and were wrapped in linguistic, cultural and conceptual terms that he felt, did not relate to him. On the other hand, when Massimo started opening up to the teachings of Marcus, Epictetus or Seneca, he felt more at home and in sync with the teachings and principles.

To Massimo, he feels plenty of people have not been exposed to Stoicism, which is why he continuously pens his thoughts on his blog, recounting his exploration with Stoicism. He states that Stoicism has changed his life for the better, so he hopes that it will also change other people's lives too. He elaborates on the ways Stoicism has changed his life. For one, he starts his day with a meditation that is influenced by a Stoic quote, followed by quiet contemplation.

He is also mindful of what happens throughout the day and ends his day retiring in a quiet corner to write his philosophical diary. Doing this daily, he feels he is much calmer and can tackle problems with more equanimity than before.

Massimo's foray into Stoicism began when we read a link to Stoic Week on his Twitter feed and thinking nothing much of it, decided to retweet it anyway. The following year was when he took a closer look to the point where he found himself co-organizing STOICON and even authoring the book 'How to Be a Stoic: Using Ancient Philosophy to Live a Modern Life.

The most important aspect of Stoicism to Massimo is its harmonious connection between practice and theory. He was always trying to live by virtues and ethics, but it wasn't until he took Stoicism seriously did he realize that this philosophy was something that he wanted to keep practicing. To Massimo, Stoicism offers a beautifully constructed, yet sufficiently flexible, mode of thought that can guide one's life day by day.

Massimo believes the Stoicism matters in today's world, the same way it mattered to the Romans and the Greeks- it helps us navigate our lives where large events take place outside of our control and in a place where we continuously seek tranquility and meaning. Human nature hasn't changed much despite the different times that we are living in.

William B. Irvine

William grew up in mining towns in Nevada and Montana. As his father was a construction engineer, he stayed in one place long enough till something was built, which was usually 12 to 18 months.

William's education began at a two-room schoolhouse that houses 1 to 3 graders and another one for 4 to 6 graders. He obtained a BA in Philosophy and Mathematics at the University of Michigan, followed by an MA and Ph.D. at UCLA in Philosophy. Post Ph.D., it was more of a nomadic career with teaching stints at the Cal State, Los Angeles than at the Pacific Lutheran University followed by the University of Cincinnati. Since 1983, Williams has been teaching at the Wright State University in Ohio.

William's research has always been focused on 'pure philosophy' on topics that were traditionally philosophical. His doctoral thesis was on phenomenalism and he continued with his first publication, "Russell's Construction of Space from Perspectives." He admits that this was the point where he lost his interest in the pure subjects and instead, focused his research on the elements that lie within the border of philosophy and 'something else.'

William's Stoical outlook look on things that other philosophers do not look at. William's practice of Stoicism is extremely close to the ancient Roman Stoics. He believes that despite the world and times changing, human nature is still very much unchanged and with

Stoicism, we humans learn how to deal with events and nature.

William's Views on Stoicism

William says that while it may be challenging to practice Stoicism at first, but when we do focus on the practice, it becomes part of our lifestyle. You experience a long stretch of tranquil living. Before he became an ardent believer in Stoicism and eventually a Stoic, William like Massimo, delved into Buddhism. At this time, he wrote the book On Desire: Why We Want What We Want (Oxford University Press, 2005) so he could take a closer look at Buddhism.

During the research of this book, William delved into human desire and among these philosophers, he looked into were the Stoic philosophers such as Seneca and Epictetus. William strives to place importance in both his academic outlook as well as his philosophical outlook for Stoicism. To him, anyone practicing Stoicism must know the ancient philosophy but also adopt these philosophies in life. Not applying Stoic practices will lead to an unhappy existence. He denounces those that study philosophy only to make a good living and not really to attain a good life.

John Sellars

Sellars attended university in 1991 pursuing philosophy. Since that time, he has always been involved with anything related to Stoicism. A large portion of his academic work focuses on peeling the many different aspects of Stoicism and its influence on society. He has written two books on Stoicism, The Art of Living and Stoicism.

John's interest in Stoicism began when he first started studying philosophy and the two main philosophers that he was most attracted to were Nietzsche and Spinoza. Nietzsche, according to Sellars, was someone who acknowledges the connection while at the same time, was very aware of the differences in Stoicism.

At the same time, Sellars was also studying Greek philosophy, which is why he has a great admiration for Socrates as well as Diogenes the Cynic. He also read Epictetus and Marcus Aurelius at the same time to understand each of these person's journey into Stoicism and when they were fully aware of their Stoic status.

Sellars View on Stoicism

One of the most important things in Stoicism that John relates to is called 'reality principle' which both Marcus and Epictetus insisted that humans face up to in finding ourselves and the human condition in general. Sellars advocates that we cannot control every element of our lives and when bad things happen, we must just accept it. Like many of the Stoics mentioned here, Sellars also feels that the issues discussed by Seneca or Marcus or Epictetus continue to be relevant to this day. These issues, according to Sella are issues that relate and reflect any person at any point, which is why reading their works can benefit the potential Stoic or those who are looking for a sense of direction.

While he doesn't think everyone should become a Stoic, he does feel that modern society can read their works and open up the possibility of addressing the issues that they are facing. This is also a way of reconnecting with the conventional tradition of thought that has played a vital part in Western culture for so many decades. He points out that plenty of people exposed to Stoicism for the first time are struck by how familiar some of the ideas are, perhaps unaware of the influence Stoicism has had on so many different parts of our shared culture.

Sellars practices Stoicism by having several sustained periods, just reading Stoic authors over the past twenty years. He does not doubt that he has been internalizing this all the way and credits Seneca's On the Shortness of Life for helping him fight procrastination on more than one occasion.

Chapter 6

Disciplines of Stoicism

From the very beginning, Stoicism has always emphasized on the categories of philosophical discourse and these categories have been divided into three themes, which are 'Ethics,' 'Physics' and 'Logic.' These discourses have roots and foundations into almost every possible Stoicism principle.

Before we go on, a note to say that philosophy itself was unified, to begin with, but theoretical discourse in the Stoic sense would be responsible for categorizing philosophy in this way which is why Stoicism is known for its three major elements.

So far the only Stoic teacher whose work survived in large amounts to this day is Epictetus'. You can find four volumes of Discourses still available for reference and use in our modern-day society. Unfortunately, for the other four volumes, it is lost. Modern Stoics also have a more compressed version of these teachings, which are compiled in Enchiridion. Epictetus lived four centuries after the founder of Stoicism, Zeno. By the time of Epictetus' death, formal Stoic schools have begun ceasing to exist.

Epictetus was the only one who chiefly defined and described the three disciplines of Stoicism and this is something scholars of today cannot find in any other Stoic literature. In this chapter, we will discuss the three disciplines, which are:

- "The Discipline of Desire," relating to the acceptance of faith and fate
- "The Discipline of Action," relating to the love of mankind or philanthropy
- "The Discipline of Assent," concerning mindfulness and how we judge things

Emperor Marcus Aurelius was taught by philosophers who were also heavily influenced and taught by Epictetus. Marcus, Stoicism' best known modern readers unfortunately never got to meet the man. Discourses, recorded by Arrian, was given to Marcus by one of his teachers as part of the study material.

In plenty of ways, Marcus has referred to these teachings which you can see in The Meditations and it also goes to show how Marcus was chiefly influenced by this particular strain of Stoicism.

Marcus uses extensively the Three Disciplines that are elaborated in Discourses, which also provides one of the main elements to interpret his very own writings.

How do we interpret Stoic disciplines?

Pierre Hadot, the French scholar, wrote an in-depth assessment of Meditations in his book called The Inner Citadel in 1998. In this book, Pierre examines in great detail the Three Disciplines while at the same time utilizing it as a framework for his exposition.

If we were to use Hadot's interpretation as a guide, then you would be able to have a clear and comprehensive framework for understanding Stoicism' teachings.

By now, you should already know that the philosophy of Stoic living was to live following nature or to live harmoniously with it.

Hadot states that all three disciplines are created to help all those who are looking to live in harmony and also combining all these three disciplines gives you the secret to a harmonious and serene path of life, with practical philosophy as the new way of living wisely.

#1 The Discipline of Desire

As indicated by Hadot, the train of "desire" is the use of day by day living of the Stoic hypothetical theme of "material science," which incorporates the Stoic investigation in normal logic, religious philosophy, and cosmology.

The discipline concerning desire is the application of living in agreement with the laws of nature. It is a universal concept and in line with the readings and dialects of religious Stoic philosophy, which is with God or with Zeus. In the discipline of Desire, this involves employing a state of mind that is philosophical, which is geared towards the existence and acknowledgment of Fate as an important and unavoidable aspect of life.

This discipline is enticing to see especially as it involves the cardinal ethics related to restraint over the silly interests, which are "strength," or perseverance despite dread and enduring, and "self-discipline" (balance), or the capacity to revoke desire and refuse false or undesirable joys.

'Amor Fati' is what Hadot calls the objective of this discipline or the acknowledgment of one's destiny. This train of thought is summed up in a standout amongst the most striking sections from the Enchiridion: "Look not for occasions to occur as you wish but rather wish occasions to occur as they do and your life will go easily and peacefully."

Cato of Utica, the Stoic hero, was known for his famous march with the surviving Republican armed forces. These armed forces marched valiantly through the hot African deserts together with Cato to make a last-ditch attempt and a brazen call against the tyrannous Julius Caesar, who looked to oust the Republic and announce himself the righteous ruler of Rome.

Despite losing the war, Cato would still become a legend in Rome and even the Stoics declared him "the invincible Cato". Invincible all because of his strong determination when it came to being conquered. Cato rather detached his intestines with his bare hands than faced the prospect of Ceasar's ruling. He was sure he would be abused and beaten under Caesar's rule; he took it upon himself to die in the most honorable way, which is why he is a legend in Rome.

Marcus Aurelius, centuries later would also lead his weakened army into battle to defend and protect Rome against barbarian hordes. Despite a devastating plague, plenty of misfortunes and invades, Marcus prevailed to victory. Should he had failed, Rome would be no more. As we'll see, the discipline of action clarifies this odd oddity: by what method can the Stoics join acknowledgment with such popular perseverance and gallant activity for the sake of equity?

#2 The Discipline of Action (Stoic Philanthropy)

The discipline of action is the utilization of daily Stoic living according to the theoretical topic of 'Ethics,' which focuses on the life goal of fulfillment or happiness - eudaimonia.

Eudaimonia relates to the Good Life, which all Stoics want to achieve. In the Discipline of Action, it involves the detailing of the

Stoic principles concerning virtues of courage, justice, self-discipline as well as wisdom. This discipline is based on the fundamentals of Stoicism doctrine, which relates to the one true good and the one true good that Stoics believe in is virtue. This is sufficient enough for any Stoic to lead a good life and to attain Eudaimonia.

Stoic ethics also cover vices such as irrational and unhealthy passions, craving, fear, emotional pain, and false pleasures. According to Hadot's view, the discipline of action is the basic ideals of living in concordance with the group of all humanity, which implies generously wishing all of humankind to thrive and accomplish "joy" (eudaimonia) the objective of life.

As we also know in Stoicism, another person's wellbeing is not within our control so we must always seek to wish them well, with the Stoic's reverse clause, which seeks to add a caveat of 'Fate permitting' or 'God willing.' As it were, Stoics do their best to act with prudence while tolerating the result of their activities to some degree disengaged way, regardless of whether achievement or disappointment. Additionally, Stoics must act as indicated by their reasonable examination of which outside results are normally to be favored. Subsequently, Marcus Aurelius seems to allude to three clauses that Stoics ought to be consistently careful to connect to the majority of their activities:

- that they are undertaken "with a reserve clause"
- that they are "for the common welfare" of mankind
- that they "accord with value"

#3 The Discipline Stoic Mindfulness

When we talk about Stoic mindfulness, we talk about Assent. Assent concerns the need to apply the daily Stoic ideas of living following Stoic logic.

Stoicism logic relates to the elements of what we now know as 'psychology' or 'epistemology.' This discipline is the virtue of living in harmony, not just with nature but with rationalization, truthfulness as well as no hidden desires in our actions, mannerism, speech, and thoughts.

It's enticing to see this teaching as specially connected with the cardinal Stoic righteousness of "knowledge" or honesty. According to Hadot, this objective of this discipline is known as the 'inner citadel' as it involves consistent awareness of our true selves as well as the capacity of the mind that is responsible for action and judgment.

Our rational thinking is where our virtue and freedom resides and this is the ultimate in the good in life. As indicated by Hadot's investigation, even though the Stoics allude to "judgment" when all is said and done (hypolêpsis), they're fundamentally inspired by checking and assessing their verifiable esteem judgments.

These ideas create the foundations of our desires, emotions, and actions, especially the vices and irrational passions that the Stoics strive to overcome.

Continuously monitoring their judgments enables Stoics to look out for early-warning symptoms that could influence impressions that are unhealthy and upsetting. By seeing this earlier on, Stoics can prevent rather than get carried away by these vices.

The Stoics call this prosochê or "attention" to the ruling capacity of the mind, to our judgments and actions.

Conclusion

As you can most likely observe, these three disciplines cover extensively and are entwined, much the same as the three conventional subjects of Stoic theory, which Hadot claims they're founded on Logic, Ethics, and Physics. In unison, the Stoic can work towards a more harmonious way of life, which is consistent with nature.

A life in service, according to the Stoics is the natural goal of human natures and the fulfillment of 'eudaimonia' which can only be achieved when you perfect moral excelling and reasoning according to the primary virtues of justice, courage, wisdom, and self-discipline.

Chapter 7

Stoicism in Relationships

To start a conversation about Stoicism and how you can use it in your relationship today, we need to look at Lucius Seneca, an entrepreneur who became a statesman in ancient Rome. Seneca was a philosopher who studied and practiced the disciplines of Stoicism. His life began from humble beginnings and he rose to become one of Rome's wealthiest and most powerful people at that time. Some say he is akin to a modern-day investment banker.

While it is hard to classify what exactly he was back in the day, Seneca can be seen as an entrepreneur who slowly but surely built his fortune, but who also lost most of it and then faced exile for many years before finally returning to Rome. He again started building his fortune. Towards the peak of his wealth, he has become more of a venture capitalist for the Roman state. He tutored the Roman Emperor Nero and was also looked highly upon as one of the wisest Roman men.

Seneca captures the joys of parenting in this writing, clearly demonstrating his love for his family, despite losing his only child. Cato, famously known for Julius Caesar also had great affection for his daughter and Epictetus, another towering Roman Stoic who pushes forth the notion that only lovers of wisdom and rationality can truly understand and appreciate love.

Back to Seneca. His immense popularity and success only turned him into the enemy of the state and towards his death, he faced execution for the crime of being too good. Nero, who eventually became a corrupt emperor would sentence Seneca to die, without thinking and Seneca was, in fact, a master of long-term thinking.

He would strategize to ensure how his teachings would survive and continue growing even after he was gone. He was acutely aware that the state would confiscate and destroy his writings and teachers and he knew he needed to make this antifragile. Seneca compiled his teachings and philosophies into letters which he mailed to specific friends such as Lucilius. These letters would become known as the *Letters from a Stoic,* or sometimes called *Seneca's Epistles.*

Loving Those We Have Properly, While We Still Can

Seneca, in the letter IX of *Seneca's Epistles,* writes and relays his admiration for the story of Stilbo, who was also a practicing Roman Stoic. As a practicing Stoic, he would go through an occasional mental practice of writing things off or even preparing in advance for the possibility of a loss of things. This practice of considering losing what we love and who we love is essentially stoic. It makes us face the present moment with gratitude and it also forces us to engage and ensure that we value those we love today properly while we still have them.

In this letter, Seneca tells a story to illustrate this point with much sympathy and admiration. He begins the story with a stoic named Stilbo who has been traveling far away from home. When Stilbo returned home, he found that barbarians had sacked his city, his entire family killed and his wife dead. Stilbo, in assessing the damaged city was asked 'What have you lost?' to which he answered 'Nihil perditi. Omnia mea mecum sunt!" Or, in English:

"I HAVE LOST NOTHING. MY GOODS ARE ALL WITH ME."

At first, you may think that this response and even Seneca's praise of it is extremely cold. However, to understand the deeper meaning of this reaction, we have to look into the Stoic principle on relationships and life. We must acknowledge that the Stoics had an ideal mental state when they pursued life. This state was apatheia.

The State of Apatheia

Apatheia translates more closely to 'Equanimity.' Apatheia is known as the mental state of being undisturbed by lesser emotions. It is a state where nothing can be removed from us because we have properly valued each and everything, including the people while they were with us.

In the state of apatheia, we do not allow petty annoyances and passions to direct our aims. We accept that we will face losses and that disturbing and distressing events will happen. It is through the recognition that we are prompted to place the right value on our loved ones while they are still around. The Stoics realized that the most consistent and prudent solution to alleviate the stinging bite of future losses was to focus on the ability to rightly value and be content with the relationships that we currently have.

This story that Seneca talks about in his letters to Lucilius is a poignant reminder of this Stoic principle and it also means that the value in Stilbo's story will not be forgotten in history.

Few Thoughts on Apatheia

Apatheia is not an easily attainable element for most of us. As humans, we will find it impossible to value everything and everyone adequately in the present. However, apatheia is still a goal that you need to work towards because of specific reasons and that has to do with lofty goals.

Lofty goals tend to push us towards achieving greater feats and when we fight hard to accomplish what is at first seem impossible, we find ourselves achieving it or we expand our definition of what is possible. When we are not afraid to cultivate our massive goals, we are elevated to achieve much more than we if had been reasonable with our goals.

Being reasonable or realistic defines your useful purpose. Anyone who dares to pursue the state of apatheia is rewarded with more meaning and purpose than what they thought they have gained. In the pursuit of higher goals, we find a higher degree of satisfaction as well as blissful contentment. This pursuit of the unattainable quietly channels us to make better progress, every single day.

Thank You, Next

You may have heard about Ariana Grande (or if you haven't, look her up). She is a singer whose song Thank You, Next, a break-up anthem is about her most recent relationships. Instead of singing about a broken heart, she sings about how each of these relationships has helped her and taught her pain, self-care as well as patience.

This is what apatheia is about when it comes to relationships. This continuous struggle for progress is the only way we can look back on our past and be satisfied with what we have achieved throughout. The pursuit of apatheia in our present context means that we create a bank of positive memories which we can always hold on to and reflect to know that we have lived a well-lived life and as we grow older (and wiser), these golden memories make up the memories for our old age.

When it comes to relationships, this pursuit of apatheia is to look back at all our relationships, whether good or bad and realize that it is, in fact, a life full of worthy experiences. No matter what fate brings us, these relationships have been of value and it is good in all of them.

In relationships, apatheia also leads us towards curiosity and growth, helping us to spark better connections and have meaningful conversations.

The Stoic Love

The Stoic love is governed by the idea of a future loss or even a potential betrayal or even the reality that our very own feelings for a person may change over time. To accept these basic conditions makes life a little more manageable when the inevitable does happen. The Stoics, being a lover of virtue, recognizes the virtue in other people.

The Stoic lover will prioritize giving love over receiving it. The Stoic lover can relinquish this love of the specific. Individualized love is important, but it is not the be-all and end-all for the essence of love. Taking this idea, the Stoic approaches love like a General in the army, equipped with a cool head and a strategic plan. He or she carries out the antidotes of Romantic excess; they are ready to love but will not fall in love. If they do fall in love, as we all humans are inclined to do, they are a way of how to pick themselves up again.

The Practice of Virtues

Stoicism is about two elements:

- The improvement of our character and to become the best version of ourselves
- The realization that much of what happens in this world is outside our control which means we need to constantly recalibrate our expectations about the universe, about life and just about everything else

These principles have a direct influence on the way Stoics view love.

Firstly, with character, the Stoics realize that the best way to improve our character is mindfully practicing the cardinal virtues of Stoicism:

- Practical wisdom- which is the ability to navigate complex situations as best as possible
- Courage- to always do the right thing

- Justice- so we are always aware of what the right is
- Temperance- everything is done in reasonable measure

This practice of four virtues is compatible with various views of love and relationships. We can be monogamous as well as polyamorous, have consensual open relationships or consensual closed relationships, to have sex for procreation or specifically for pleasure.

None of these virtues implies that a person lacks practical wisdom, temperance, courage or justice. There are, however, certain things that are always and clearly out of bounds such as cheating on your partner. This is a case of injustice, intemperance as well as cowardice. For a Stoic, this is a definite no-no.

Similarly, if sex is seen as not just a mutually pleasurable activity to share with your partner and only an obsession or a chief pursuit in its way, then this is seen as being the opposite of being virtuous.

Pleasure and a Loving Relationship

Pleasure, for the Stoic, is another preferred indifferent. It is preferable to pain or in the absence of pleasure as long as it does not get in the way of our virtue. Love is not the same as pleasure.

A loving relationship should always be pleasurable for both parties, but when we talk about pleasure, it is often the physical, the emotional as well as the intellectual. However, if the context of pleasure if given precedence of the love share, then this is a problem that results in the couple or the person losing their ethical bearings.

What about the things that are not in our control? As Epictetus put it, some things are within our control and some are not. What is within our power is opinion, desire, motivation, and aversion, basically everything that we do.

That said, whatever that is not within our power does not mean we cannot influence it.

In this context, what does that have to do with love?

We all want to be loved, but according to the Stoics, this thinking is a huge mistake because other people's feelings, their actions as well as their judgments are not within our control.

Instead, we should focus on being the most lovable person for our companion and whether they return this favor or not, it is up to them. We need to do our utmost best. Wanting to control people and the events outside our reach only leads to misery and pain.

For example, the feeling of jealousy is sometimes inevitable in relationships. If we are jealous, it is usually one of two things:

- You do not trust your lover
- You are attempting to control something (their behavior) that is outside your sphere of action.

When this happens, you end up becoming miserable and it also will be miserable as well. When you decide to get a grip on your feelings, what you are doing here is being reasonable and project positive emotions and not suppressing your emotions. You are just trying to look at things in a more objective light.

Stoicism teaches us to become better humans by modulating our natural perceptions, desires, and emotions. It teaches us how to become better and act accordingly.

Love Everything that Happens

Another good principle in Stoicism is called the "art of acquiescence", to accept rather than fight every little thing.

In most events or scenarios that have taken place especially those that have gone south, we can only change our opinions on them and not the event itself, unless we had a time machine and could go back in time. So, we can only accept what has happened and look forward to these two steps:

- To accept that we don't control everything that happens. We simply must accept it.
- To not only accept, but even love everything that happens. We simply get to enjoy it. It is hard to feel grateful or happy for something that we never wanted to take place, but things happen for a reason and whether it is the desired effect or an unexpected outcome, it happened specifically for you.

You may not understand why it happened, but eventually, you will and you will see how it benefited you.

Our Greatest Asset is our Willpower

Apart from our willpower, we also have other strong assets, which are our decision making and our discipline.

Most of us would not be where we are today if it not had been for our discipline, hard work and our ability to change our circumstances.

We have been accustomed to the fact that by doing right or doing good, the universe will respond in goodness too and it will do what we hope it would do so things will more or less go our way.

Is this true? Do you think this way?

But what if things do not happen the way expect it to? Do we just accept it?

Yes. Yes, exactly.

Psychologist Albert Ellis points out our tendency to not accept this but instead of object it. We must move away from the perception and thinking that things must be the way we want them or must be the way we expected.

Stuff will happen to us in life, but it is up to us to choose which ones we want to be okay with and which wants to want to resist. People are going to be a certain way; events will occur as they do. But it isn't just life events.

The solution to all of this is not to fight it with incredible amounts of energy. As Epictetus put it:

Do not seek to have events happen as you want them, but instead, want them to happen and your life will go well.

The Art of Acquiescence

The Stoics referred to the idea above as the art of acquiescence. Abraham Lincoln's favorite quotes pretty much sum it by - And this too shall pass. This is where acceptance is needed.

You may not have to like what is happening to work with current situations, but you can use it to your advantage. However, it starts by looking at the situation clearly and accepting what is happening wholeheartedly. Because that's your only option. The Stoics also used another metaphor called Logos, which is the universal guiding force.

The notion here is that we can struggle with the situation and try our best to challenge it or we can go along for the ride and enjoy it, and along the way learn and make notes to change your situation when the tide changes too.

Amor Fati

The thing is, we need to go through setbacks in various forms to do great things. Remember that it is pressure that creates a diamond and agitation in an oyster that creates a pearl. We need to love the things we do and sometimes accept what happens as a result, whether it is good or bad. We have to learn to find joy in every single thing that happens.

Once we discard our expectations and accept what happens, there is the moment of understanding that some things (especially bad things) are beyond our control. At this point, we need to love whatever that has happened to us and face forward ahead in life with unfailing cheerfulness. Indifference and acceptance are better than rage and disappointment. Very few people practice this, but it is only the first step.

We do not get to choose what happens to us, but we can always choose how we feel about it. You want to feel good- even if this good feeling does not happen immediately after a bad situation, we will still strive to move towards feeling good and feeling happy. If the event must occur, Amor fati (a love of fate) is the response. Do not waste to ponder even for a second looking at your expectations that did not happen. Face forward, and face it with a smug little grin.

Chapter 8

Stoicism in Business

When it comes to business, nobody wants to fail. We all want to avoid doing as many mistakes as possible, especially rookie ones to ensure that our losses are little to none. Unfortunately, the best way to learn is to fail. Failure is after all our friends in disguise.

That said, understanding all there is to know about the business you are in and equipping yourself with the right know-how, knowledge, expertise, and trends will help you avoid glaring pitfalls.

As the 21st century goes on, business trends move towards a swirling interest around resilience, mindfulness, and innovation to overcome pitfalls and mistakes. Many have trodden this path, leaving us with many lessons for us to learn.

Among these lessons is the brand of ancient western philosophy that is Stoicism. Stoicism focuses on mindfulness as well as resilience. It focuses on the mindset that enables us to flourish and live the Good Life as well as achieving Eudemonia. These guiding principles have had a significant impact on Western ideology and thought process.

Stoicism in business helps us to overcome destructive emotions. Here we again focus on the three most famous Stoics of ancient Rome and derive lessons we can use and practice in business.

- Marcus Aurelius- focused on compassion, humility, and restraint in life
- Epictetus- overcame the horrors of slavery, going on to find his school of thought
- Seneca- though faced with death from Emperor Nero, was focused on ensuring the comforts of his wife and friends.

At the very core of their teachings are three basic lessons:

- The world is volatile and predictable and life is brief
- We need to be steadfast, strong and in control of ourselves
- Dissatisfaction arises from our impulsive actions rather than a logic course

If you are looking for a prime example of Stoicism in business as well as in leadership, look no further than the previous Commander-in-Chief, former President Barack Obama who is very obvious in demonstrating stoic qualities through his calm and collected demeanor. Many say that his behavior patterns echo that of Roman stoic, Cato the Younger.

To be stoical is to transform negative emotions into a perspective that prepares you to be in the right state of mind because as well know, our mind, our actions, our reactions are the only things within our control and we ditch the other things that we have no grasp on.

To be stoical in business is to be aware, in control as well as be mindful of what we do, who we engage with, the trends in our industry, expenditure and the day-to-day running of our business entities. We train our minds to be this way rather than get lost in the various emotions and random thought processes that lead us to lose focus on our business goals.

The Stoic exercise, such as practicing misfortune and poverty, really helps business owners to prepare for worst-case scenarios rather than just going into a fall sense of success that everything is alright.

When this happens, when we fall into a dull lull, we make no preparations in case the stock market crashes, we do not work on making enough savings, we do not diversify our business plans and most importantly, we do not innovate.

Practicing stoic principles into our business and entrepreneurship as well as in our leadership can help us build resilience and change our state of mind to rebound from knockbacks.

Another Stoic principle is to turn problems into opportunities. If you want to cultivate a culture of creativity in your business, then you need to think of 'The Glass half Full, instead of half-empty' and to turn obstacles upside down. Look for an opportunity in every bad situation.

Stoics Lessons for Business, for Leadership

1) Rationality, perspective, and logic

We need to control ourselves first before we reach out to control the events that are happening around us. Self-control is the only thing that will bring success every time.

2) Authenticity

While having role models to look up to is healthy, however,

emulation can turn into imitation and all you will ever produce is a second-rate product with no ounce of innovation. Stoicism here helps us in embracing our unique quirks and using it to leverage into our business.

3) Self-mastery and purposeful action

A Stoic will know exactly what they want from the get-go. They have clear goals with clear routes to get there. You can channel this by writing your daily goals because when you do this, you create a psychological pre-commitment on what you need to do the minute you wake up and you also create a self-expectation that increases the likelihood of achieving these tasks.

Science continues to prove what the Stoics have known for all these centuries. According to Shawn Achor, a psychologist at Harvard, professionals who worked on gratitude practice each start of their day performed at a much efficient and productive level than those who did not. They also achieved a higher dopamine release that boosted their overall performance, happiness, and mood.

4) Military leaders follow their principles

In 1965, when James Stockdale's plane was shot down over Vietnam, he told himself, 'At least I'm leaving the world of tech and entering the world of Epictetus.' Not something you would have thought of in the event you found yourself in this scenario. Stockdale would spend over 7 years in a Vietnamese prison and during this time, he wrote about Stoicism and how it saved his life. He is quoted as saying "You must never confuse faith that you will prevail in the end—which you can never afford to lose—with the discipline to confront the most brutal facts of your current reality, whatever they might be."

5) Stoicism is ideal for the entrepreneur

As an entrepreneur, having to practice misfortune makes you a stronger person with a stronger mindset, which helps you overcome adversity. You are better able to flip obstacles upside down, turning problems into opportunity and also keeping a perspective of how small you are; you also keep your ego manageable.

6) Stoicism lends itself to globalization

Epictetus shared the poignant reminder- that each of us is a citizen in our land, but we are also members of the great city of gods and men'. Marcus Aurelius consistently reminded himself to love the world.

As we all rush to meet the changes of this world and continue creating innovations to make this world a better place to live in, we can look towards Stoicism to give us a system that we can cultivate and take relief from what the Stoics call ' a personal operating system for a high-pressured environment.'

We hope this chapter has given you an understanding and a powerful antidote to help you maneuver your way through life and in business

As Marcus Aurelius remarked:

"THE THINGS YOU THINK ABOUT DETERMINING THE QUALITY OF YOUR MIND."

Chapter 9

Stoicism in School

If we understand Epictetus's teaching correctly, a sign of the educated is based on the knowledge of the difference between what is within one's control and what is not.

In this chapter, we focus solely on educators. It would be extremely helpful for educators to learn this difference in their professional careers because it will help them to create more fruitful relationships with their students, produce more effective teaching, lessen the burden and mental stress they face as well as prevent any psychological burnout. If we look at Epictetus to help us navigate Stoicism in the educational sphere, then it would help educators become more rational pessimists and expect more will go wrong than right.

Staying Stoical in School

Some of the most profound questions asked when it comes to education and life is:

- What is the best way to live?
- How can we deal with the difficult situations that we face?
- What would it take to improve our minds?

If you have questions like these, then the answers to this lie at the very base of Stoic philosophy. Educators in schools, colleges, and institutions can use their insights on adversity, on the mind as well as on practice to help our students shape the way they think and cultivate a positive thought pattern.

Some two thousand years ago, a teacher, a playwright, and an emperor asked:

Stoicism in school

In school, children learn how to deal with difficult emotions such as worry, frustration, cravings, fear, arguments, temper, gossip, squabbles, jealousy, bitterness, hurt and many other complex emotions. Through stoicism, we can offer more fortifying ways to think about dealing with these difficulties:

Teachers can …

- Show students the things that are always within their control, which are their responses to situations, their thoughts as well as their reactions.
- Show and teach pupils how to anticipate as well as cope with adversity
- Guide students on how they can change their perceptions so that they resent less complain less. It will also help them to instill and keep a positive perspective, stay grateful, and be happy.

Pupils can learn how to…

- Let go of frustration by realizing that their minds are within their control and they can let go of the irritation that is counterproductive to their goals. This should be released and not dwelt on.

- Let go of unnecessary worries by remembering that the more they worry about things that are outside their control, the worse they will feel. On the other hand, the less they worry, the happier and calmer they are.
- Cope with arguments by avoiding incessant complaining, avoiding criticizing as well as blaming or resenting the people around them. Instead, they can focus on endeavors and feelings of gratefulness and cheerfulness.

School leaders can convey the lives of the thinkers, and their thinking …

By looking at the leaders of Roman Stoicism, senior leadership teams and leaders can set the foundation of a cohesive and fruitful mind that focuses on things, elements and experiences that are controlled by our selves.

Epictetus, Marcus Aurelius, and Lucius Seneca were all thinkers who used mantras, analogies as well as writing in diaries, letters, and notebooks. All three were leaders who were also tutors and advisors.

Their main analogies:

Slavery: The irritation that enslaves us whereas wisdom frees us

Illusions: The anxieties that are the products of our creation and which is something we can get rid of Boxing: To continuously train hard, so we do not let these anxieties bring us down.

Introducing Stoicism to your Students

In their first week of school, you can teach them the approach to life and that everyone experiences difficulties, but we all have it in us to overcome these difficulties. You can do this in assemblies or an hour of lesson. You can also discuss this over a group. With stoicism, you teach your students to anticipate the frustrations of life as well as the mantra 'Stay Stoical.'

Here are 6 ways you can use Stoicism in exams, during detention, in arguments, in pain, in sports and also in communicating with your student's families:

- In detention … stay stoical!

Oftentimes, students will feel upset or even resent your giving them detention. In your conversations with them, remind them to stay stoical, calm as well as help them build and keep a perspective of their detention. Teach them to let go of anger, work out the elements that they can control as well as think about how they can build trust in the future. You can also allow them to decide what they want to do differently next time.

- Before, in and after exams … stay stoical!

Of course, tests can be extremely stressful for both children, their parents, as well as the teachers, creating and marking these tests. For students, educators can help them see that preparing, revising and overcoming their procrastination is something that is within their control. If they do fail an exam or perform poorly, remember to tell them to remain stoical and not to allow this minor complication agitate them. Instead, tell them to focus on what they can do differently the next time around and help them with their upcoming assessments.

- In arguments … stay stoical!

When a student gets into an argument with their fellow students or friends, using stoicism here can help to remind both parties to practice calm, ignore vicious rumors as well as ignore gossip and insults. It also helps them to stay positive or rational rather than give in to these negative thoughts and exacerbate anger and mistrust.

- When ill or struggling… stay stoical!

It is a struggle to wake up early and get to school and it is even harder if students are feeling ill. Of course, if they are feeling well but lack the motivation to get up and come to school, use stoicism to help them see that waking up anyway, showing up anyway is something to be proud of. Help students see that some setbacks can be controlled. If they fall, get back up and try again. If they colored outside the lines, then create your masterpiece. The idea here is that a stoic mindset reduces our fragility. The volatility of the world itself cannot destabilize us. With the use of stoicism, problems can become opportunities as long as we train our resilience.

- At sport … stay stoical!

Sports are competitive by nature and at times, tempers can run high. The use of stoicism here can help students not to over-celebrate their wins and jeer those who did not win a match or score a goal. On the other hand, not winning also teaches us not to despair or put on the blame game. Using stoicism prevents a footballer from turning a yellow card into a red card or from getting a contestant from being disqualified. If there are any setbacks, great- here's a chance to train our willpower.

- With your families … stay stoical!

Growing up, children also face difficult times. As much as we would like to shelter them from the adversities of life, children also face issues and problems of their own with their friends, peers, siblings, and cousins. If they are taught to remain stoical in school, then they can cascade these learnings to their own family life by enabling them to deal with arguments and adversity in their families such as death or divorce. It gives them a good perspective and enables them to remain grateful and not take the people around them for granted. Rather, they develop meaningful relationships with their immediate family members, which then transcends into their adult lives.

Teaching children to remain stoic during tough times creates a powerful perspective for them that helps them to improve their resilience, their relationships and also their lives.

Chapter 10

Seeing the Glass Half Full

In stoicism, you see the world as it is an attempt to not try and change a person's view of things. Simultaneously, stoics also try to work on their minds to act in a way that they will be proud of.

Before we go into the Stoic's idea of the glass half full, here are the various ways in which other philosophies and religion see the glass half full, just to give you an idea:

- Buddhism: The glass doesn't exist, for nothing does.
- Solipsism: I am the glass. And the whole world is nothing but my alcoholic delirium.
- Islam: There is no glass except glass.
- Judaism: Why only my glass is half empty?
- Orthodoxy: The glass is half empty as a punishment for our sins.
- Catholicism: The glass is half empty only for bad people.
- Freudianism: You were underserved as a child.
- Stoicism: Yes. My glass is half-empty, and I deserve it to be so.
- Communism: Everyone is entitled to a full glass.
- Socialism: Yes, the glass is only half full. But it is equally so for everyone.
- Yoga: You are both the glass and its contents. You and your glass are One.

- Science: The glass contains 1/2 of liquid and 1/2 of air, thus the glass is always full.

When we talk about how an optimist views a glass of water, we usually normally their thought process but saying they look at the glass as being half full.

For a Stoic, the level of optimism is only the starting point. The stoic, after expressing their appreciation that the glass is half full will then go on to express their delight in having a glass. Because, that glass could have been chipped, broken or stolen.

And if they are bringing their Stoic philosophy in, the Stoic might even go so far as to say that glass vessels are a unique thing. Not only are they cheap but also durable and above all, allows us to see the contents inside. The stoic representation of the glass sounds a bit extensive or silly but take note of how they have given their perspective on it. The stoic shares their capacity of joy and in doing so, have shown you that the world is indeed, a wonderful place.

To a stoic, the glass is amazing, but to everyone else around them, the glass is just another glass and it is a glass that is half empty.

According to William B. Irvine, author of the Book 'A Guide to the Good Life: The Ancient Art of Stoic Joy', the first order of business to understand Stoicism is to realize that in English, stoic means emotionless but it is such a huge difference to the Greek understanding and practice. Stoic, in the Greek sense, is to have elements of tranquility. One can say that it is similar to Buddhism, albeit without Buddhism's insistence of detaching the positive and joyous elements.

So how can the average person practice this aspect of Stoicism- of looking at the glass not only as half full but also as a wonderful thing?

Here are six ways you to see the glass as half full:

#1 Stop comparing yourself to others.

The world is not always about you. It never was about you. When a neighbor gets a new car or a friend gets a raise or your colleague loses weight and none of this reflects on yourself, don't fret! Just because you did not get any of those, does not mean you never will. You still have time to improve yourself. All of us hit different milestones in life at different periods. Some people get married earlier while some get married later in life, some people end up buying a house before their 30s while you only bought yours at the age of 40. You graduate on time while some friends did not. When we compare ourselves to the people around us, we usually feel worthless and end up not performing to the best of our abilities because we think we've run out of time.

You only run out of time when you are on your deathbed.

#2 Change your focus.

Pessimism and optimism are just nothing more than average feelings we all go through. If you are moping about and wondering why your life sucks, you are bound to be feeling more pessimistic about things. However, use the Stoic approach to shift your perspective and look at the glass full or even the fact that there is a glass and there are contents in it. When you shift your thoughts to something that involves more gratitude, you will feel much more optimistic about the situation you are in and you might also find ways and ideas to better yourself.

#3 Look for positive signs everywhere.

Again, it's all about perception. Look for the good in things and you'll see that you can smile a little bit more. See something that triggers a happy memory? Be grateful. Found a penny on the floor? Pick it up and be grateful. It takes very little to be happy but enormous energy to be sad.

#4 Listen to uplifting music.

If you find yourself having a bad day or for some reason just feeling pessimistic and down, listen to feel-good music. 'Happy' by Pharrell Williams is music so uplifting it is hard not to tap your feet to the sound of the beat. Josh Groban's 'You Raise Me Up' is another motivational music that can help literally, lift you. Music does have the power to heal so if you ever feel that you are in a pessimistic frame of mind, put some good music on and shake to the rhythm as this will help shift your negative feelings to a positive one.

#5 Detach from outcomes.

The root of optimism lies in knowing that when one opportunity passes, another one will come. As much as we think that that was our window or moment, sometimes there is a reason why we let it go. It may seem to others around you that it was the perfect opportunity for you to act or be in or sign up or explore, but maybe you weren't ready that is why you did not act upon it?

Take a look at your life before this and identify the times where you wanted something but did not get it but looking back, you are glad that things turned out the way it did for you.

#6 Stop saying you are a pessimist.

Words, like music, are a powerful thing. When you start thinking of yourself as good or kind or optimistic, you radiate a good vibe about yourself. People around you feel it and eventually- this becomes who you are. Mention your name and people say you're great to be around with or you're the life of the party or that you are such a positive force to the team. What you feel and think and say will become part of who you are.

Conclusion

This goes to say that always being happy or seeing the glass half full is always good, being optimistic all day, every day may distract you from negative things that are happening around you and prevent you from acting appropriately. Case in point, if someone has lost a family member, you react by giving your condolences and not to say tomorrow is a better day. We need balance at the end of the day and this chapter serves to look at ways to believe in yourself and be optimistic.

Chapter 11

Techniques for Using Stoicism in Daily Life

If you are interested in leading a life based on Stoic principles, then here are some exercises that you can do to develop Stoic practices and outlooks. These exercises can benefit potential Stoic but also be extremely helpful to anyone doing these exercises.

Just keep in mind that Stoicism is a philosophy of life and not something that enables you to achieve spiritual enlightenment. Therefore, these exercises can be used by anyone in this life. They are practical and they also do not need any kind of special tools or equipment, except determination and a functioning brain.

#1 Early Morning Reflection

Early morning reflection has been known to have plenty of benefits and it is greater than just being about planning what you want to do on that day. It is also about your reaction to these things and how others will react as well. You anticipate the things that would take place.

One of the first few things to do in your reflection is grateful that you have woken up- not many people have this privilege today. Once done, you can then plan out how to embrace your virtues and how to avoid your vices. It doesn't have to be a detailed plan, but it is just something for you to go over.

For instance, it can be a personal strength you want to cultivate-you can think about how you will be incorporating it into your day. Do you want to procrastinate less? Do you want to avoid being part of office gossip? Do you want to arrive at meetings on time? Mentally check how you will be dealing with the difficult situations that will arrive.

Next, you want to remind yourself that only you are in control of your thoughts as well as your actions. Everything else is not your control. You can do your early morning reflection with a walk to enjoy the rising sun or you can even perform some light stretches on your bed and meditate thereafter. Some light exercises using your body weight also helps.

#2 A View from Above

The second exercise to practice is designed to remind where you are in this world and the importance you bring. We are not talking about how big a role you play in the scheme of things but really, how small you are in the course of life. How many lives can you touch being where you are now? How many people are you significant to? This is not about bringing you down and saying that your life is not as important as you thought it was, but it is about relating to the whole world and beyond.

Again, you need to meditate somewhere quit so pick a place such a park on a beach if you live near one. Otherwise, a park will do. Look above starting with the clouds and then slowly bring yourself closer to the world and people. Observe things around you from discoveries, creation, first kisses, traffic jams, the sound of the blaring horn. Observe but do not judge because now, you need to think about how you are related to all of this. How do you see yourself in these situations and know that all these things are only relatively important and that is how you are relatively important?

You are only important to a certain extent. Life existed before you and will continue to exist after you so worry yourself about things that directly involve your being.

#3 Contemplation of the Ideal Person

In this exercise, we will look at a catalyst for change towards becoming your ideal self. Becoming your ideal self is a never-ending quest. The older we get, the more things we know, the wiser we become and we find that our priorities also change. Your ideal persona will continue to change based on your experiences and lessons in life.

But for now, at this moment that you are in, what kind of person do you make yourself to be? What qualities, to you, make an ideal person?

This is not a question that has a straightforward answer. In some respects, it would be easier to ask what an ideal person would do in a situation rather than their characteristics. From the actions of this person, you can then derive their qualities and characteristics and hopefully, emulate them on your own.

You can start by creating a list of your role models, past, present ones that you had the opportunity to get to know, to work with and so on. Determine what their best qualities are and whether you want to emulate this. After all, imitation is the best form of flattery.

You can also make a list of people you do not like and what you do not like about them and then strive to avoid these characteristics.

#4 Cultivating Philanthropy

What is philanthropy? Philanthropy can be defined as a desire to promote and ensure the welfare of other people. We hear about how billionaires and celebrities are philanthropists and the kinds of things they do.

This word is often associated with rich people, people with money. But philanthropy does not only constitute money. Having the right attitude and the desire to help people is what makes a philanthropist — not the amount of money.

When we endeavor to do philanthropy, our goals need to be community-centric. It needs to be thinking about the wider scope of our work and how it can bring everyone closer, towards a common goal and a connected circle.

Your family is an extension of yourself and by another extension-the community you live in. These connections go far and wide as the entire country. Hierocles, the Stoic philosopher said we should look at our siblings as an extension of our own.

How does this benefit you; you might ask?

Thinking of yourself as part of connectivity to your family and community, you end up not becoming overly attached to any single individual. You are your person, albeit connected in some way or another. This also means you are part of a larger circle of friends, which means you are exposed to a greater set of cultures and viewpoints, giving you an incredible opportunity for learning.

So how do you extend your circle?

You can start by striking up a conversation with someone at your workplace that you barely talk to. You can say YES to a party invitation which you otherwise would have said no to because you prefer being at home. Another thing to do is to ensure that your close friends are aware that you consider them a part of your family and that you can be relied on to be there for them should they need you.

#5: Self Retreat

Self-retreat, whenever possible, is a must. Self-retreat enables you to find peace or freedom, even for a tiny bit, from the regularities of life.

Peace and freedom are the things that come from inside you, so if you are trying to run away from cognitive dissonance, then you are running away from yourself. Plenty of people feel that they need to 'go somewhere' or travel to find peace of mind.

You can if you want to, but for a cheaper alternative, peace can be found just about anywhere and it all begins with a visit into your mind. Don't get weird out. Nowhere else is anyone as free as in their mind. You can be anything you want inside your head; you can be as different as you want in your mind. While traveling is wonderful, it's not the only way to find yourself. All you need is to shut yourself out from the world, about five to 10 minutes

According to Marcus Aurelius, people seek retreats to countrysides and seashores or hills for themselves and this has become a habit

You can escape your physical or mental confinement by journeying inside your mind. Those that feel trapped by work or the responsibilities of life feel lifeless and turn into pessimists. Those that are trapped inside mental confinements move towards being depressed or worse.

One of the very best ways to journey without ever having to leave the comforts of your own home is by reading and of course, meditating.

#6 Philosophical Journal

Have you thought of keeping a journal? It could be an online journal or a private blog or you can go old school and keep a paperback journal but whatever it is, have you thought about it?

The difference with this journal is that instead of writing about your life and what has happened in it, you instead write about life from a Stoical perspective, meaning you analyze life as a way to discover your shortcomings and track the way you make changes to live according to the Good Life.

After all, constant reflection is what can improve our current circumstances as well as our outlook on the future.

By planning our actions according to an ethical framework, you can then look back and see what you can change based on the scenarios and events that took place. Did you get irritated when you did not get your answer immediately while researching something? Did you snap at the customer service representative for asking too many verification questions? Were you confused after a long meeting with your colleagues about a new project?

Analyzing your day in your Stoic journal can help you work towards changing yourself for the better. A Stoic journal can just your normal journal with an added philosophical entry.

If you want to start a Stoic journal, then best to keep going at it for 21 days (21 days is scientifically proven to cultivate and keep a habit). You can also read the philosophical journal entry by the Roman Emperor, Marcus Aurelius called 'Meditations.'

#7: Understanding That Life Has Layers

In any event or scenario, there are many different layers. Just like an onion, we can do an exercise of stripping away each layer to find out what it represents and what each individual contributes to the scenario.

What is the value that this situation holds for everyone? In most cases, there is no value.

What is the kind of skills that this event or scenario would need? It is great if you have the skills needed, but one good way of self-development is viewing the situation without interfering.

For example, let us take a look at a common rite of passage for everyone- growing up and figuring out where we fit in the scheme of things.

As we grow up, we often struggle to find or decide what we want to do in life. Some people have it easy and know immediately what they like and what their passions are and then there are the rest of us who are still trying to find something fulfilling and meaningful to work towards.

Some of us have an excellent start in life while some of us end up doing something for the sake of money and some of us do it because it is expected of us or it's the only way we know.

You know the drill. Go to school, do well, get good grades, graduate, look for a job, find a spouse, get married, have kids and then work and work and work till we die?

Some of us fit into that mold while some of us do not.

So ask yourself this- What would you do if money was not an issue? Answer this question, then work your way towards that. It doesn't mean that you need to quit your 9-5 job straight away, but the idea here is to work towards reaching that goal, incrementally.

#8 Bedtime Reflection

We started this series of exercises with a morning reflection and we end the day with a night reflection. Your reflection should focus on what has taken place in your day to day and not about what is going to happen.

Mentally go through the things that happened in your day and ask yourself if:

- Did you behave according to your principles?
- You treated the people with whom you interacted with in a friendly and considerate manner?
- What vices did you fight?
- Did you make yourself a better person by cultivating your virtues?

In your Stoic journal, you can also write down your reflections and you can also plan the next day too. Write down your notes and what you want to reflect on in the morning. What you do today will link up with tomorrow morning's reflection.

In your journal, write down what you want to improve the next day. It doesn't have to be a big thing. Write it down, no matter how small the improvement may be. If you keep this up for 21 days, you'd be surprised how much you can and would be able to change.

Along with your notes, also remind yourself that this day has ended and there is no way you can change anything about it unless you time traveled. What has happened, has happened. The sun will rise tomorrow.

#9 Negative Visualization

Negative visualization is an exercise focused on reminding us of how privileged we are, even when we think we are not. It is a simple idea, but one that has an enormous impact. All of us need to do is to imagine that terrible things have taken place or, good things have not taken place. Keep in mind that this is not an exercise steering you into negativity. It is simply giving you an idea of the scale of catastrophe:

You lost your wallet. But it could be worse - you could have lost all your possessions

You are set up on a blind date. But it could be worse- you could have married without ever meeting your spouse beforehand.

Your aunt met in an accident and is in the hospital recovering. It could be worse- she could have died.

You met with an accident and fractured your arm. It could be worse- you may have been paralyzed.

You can also imagine how situations that you are about to embark on will go wrong.

This kind of therapy is not cultivating pessimism, but instead, it makes you realize that things could get worse and things could turn bad, but it has not and it did not happen to you.

In doing this exercise, you can try and imagine some catastrophes that could take place in the act that you are about to do or the situation that you are in. Maybe you could imagine having born in a time that you would miss having the convenience of the internet or being born at a time when women were not allowed to vote? Or traveling to far off places could only be done through sailing.

#10 Physical Self-Control Training

In this exercise, we look at physical hardships and going without the stuff we enjoy. This exercise, if you look at it, is a practical version of the exercise above.

In this exercise, it serves to achieve two purposes:

- To prepare ourselves to have hardships
- To be happy with what we have and not to desire the things that are not within our control.

Everything in life should be grasped loosely, like sand through our hands. You do not hold sand tightly because if you do, it escapes your grasp.

These are a few examples that you can try in your physical self-control:

- Eating only one meal a day
- Drinking water only for a certain period
- Not having baths instead only timed showers
- Only having the option of one phone call a day

The point of doing all of the above and anything else that you can think of is that you need to view everything as a transient from yourself to the things you own to everyone you know all of this will cease to exist.

The best way forward is to view everything on a loan so instead of having to say "I have lost it," you switch your perception to "I have given it back." Reflect on your situations and realize that you did not lose anything but merely, returned it. In doing so, you also create an optimistic view.

To get started on this, you can change something in your daily routine to make your day a little harder. Maybe instead of driving to work, take the bus. Maybe instead of having your chia seed pudding, skip your breakfast and only have coffee. Maybe go without the internet for a day?

Bottom line

The exercises stated in this chapter help you cultivate Stoic thinking in a modern-day setting. You can always do two or three exercises together, such as taking a morning walk and reflecting at the same time but choosing now to wear a jacket and being grateful for the crisp morning air. You've successfully done self-control and negative visualization while going on your morning walk and reflection. Stoicism is not hard and complicated. You need to understand its values before you dismiss it. Also, you do not need to call yourself a Stoic to practice Stoicism.

The main denominator behind all of these exercises is that they only require you to take a long and hard look at yourself and the way you live your life. This is never a bad thing, no matter what viewpoint you look at life.

Conclusion

We hope you now have a better and clearer understanding of Stoicism, its disciplines, as well as its principles and how you can apply them in your daily life. You can look at this book as a means of self-realization and self-help because it does facilitate cognitive, behavioral as well as emotional improvement in your life.

Focusing on what we can control and letting go of what we cannot, to us seems to be a pretty positive way to lead our lives. Often, we let the little things get to us and with this Stoic principle in mind, it helps us stay focused on what matters.

Even practicing misfortune, in asking ourselves- what could go wrong, can not only prepare us for whatever tests that may come our way, but it also helps us troubleshoot problems in our work, in life and relationships.

As mentioned at the start of this book, the Stoic philosophy offers a broader philosophical perspective so even if you do not intend to lead a life based on the Stoic philosophy, you can still practice some of its principles to make your life better.

While Stoicism has withered away for some time, it is now coming back in its full glory, with new-age philosophers bringing in Stoicism to fit the modern world. You may not agree with all aspects of Stoicism, but the idea here is to use some of its principles to work on the areas of life that you feel need repair or need help in.

Hopefully, this book will further inspire you to read more about what the ancient philosophers have written down, such as books and writings from Seneca, Epictetus, Marcus Aurelius.

If you enjoyed this book, please let me know your opinion by leaving a short review on Amazon. Thanks!